GRAPHIC ORGANIZERS
AND OTHER
VISUAL STRATEGIES

ENGAGE THE
BRAIN

MARCIA L. TATE

CORWIN PRESS
Classroom

For information:

Corwin Press
A SAGE Publications Company
2455 Teller Road
Thousand Oaks, California 91320
CorwinPress.com

SAGE Publications, Ltd.
1 Oliver's Yard
55 City Road
London EC1Y 1SP
United Kingdom

SAGE Publications India Pvt. Ltd.
B 1/I 1 Mohan Cooperative
Industrial Area
Mathura Road, New Delhi
India 110 044

SAGE Publications Asia-Pacific Pvt. Ltd.
33 Pekin Street #02-01
Far East Square
Singapore 048763

Printed in the United States of America.

ISBN 978-1-4129-5229-3

This book is printed on acid-free paper.

08 09 10 11 12 10 9 8 7 6 5 4 3 2 1

Executive Editor: Kathleen Hex
Managing Developmental Editor: Christine Hood
Editorial Assistant: Anne O'Dell
Developmental Writer: Q. L. Pearce
Developmental Editor: Christine Hood
Proofreader: Bette Darwin
Art Director: Anthony D. Paular
Cover Designer: Monique Hahn
Interior Production Artist: Karine Hovsepian
Illustrator: Mike Wesley
Design Consultant: PUMPKiN PIE Design

GRADE **5**

TABLE OF CONTENTS

Connections to Standards

This chart shows the national academic standards that are covered in each chapter.

MATHEMATICS	Standards are covered on pages
Numbers and Operations—Understand numbers, ways of representing numbers, relationships among numbers, and number systems.	15, 18
Algebra—Represent and analyze mathematical situations and structures using algebraic symbols.	15
Geometry—Analyze characteristics and properties of two- and three-dimensional geometric shapes, and develop mathematical arguments about geometric relationships.	28
Data Analysis and Probability—Formulate questions that can be addressed with data, and collect, organize, and display relevant data to answer them.	9, 12, 22
Data Analysis and Probability—Select and use appropriate statistical methods to analyze data.	9, 12
Data Analysis and Probability—Develop and evaluate inferences and predictions that are based on data.	9, 12
Data Analysis and Probability—Understand and apply basic concepts of probability.	9, 22
Problem Solving—Apply and adapt a variety of appropriate strategies to solve problems.	25
Problem Solving—Monitor and reflect on the process of mathematical problem solving.	25
Communication—Communicate mathematical thinking coherently and clearly to peers, teachers, and others.	25
Communication—Analyze and evaluate the mathematical thinking and strategies of others.	25

SCIENCE	Standards are covered on pages
Science as Inquiry—Ability to conduct scientific inquiry.	31, 34, 37
Science as Inquiry—Understand about scientific inquiry.	34, 37
Physical Science—Understand motions and forces.	34
Life Science—Understand structure and function in living systems.	40, 44
Life Science—Understand regulation and behavior.	40
Earth and Space Science—Understand structure of the earth system.	48

SOCIAL STUDIES	Standards are covered on pages
Understand culture and cultural diversity.	55
Understand the ways human beings view themselves in and over time.	55, 58, 61
Understand the interactions among people, places, and environments.	52, 55
Understand how people create and change structures of power, authority, and governance.	64, 68
Understand the ideals, principles, and practices of citizenship in a democratic republic.	68

LANGUAGE ARTS	Standards are covered on pages
Read a wide range of print and nonprint texts to build an understanding of texts, of self, and of the cultures of the United States and the world; to acquire new information; to respond to the needs and demands of society and the workplace; and for personal fulfillment (includes fiction and nonfiction, classic, and contemporary works).	71, 80
Read a wide range of literature from many periods in many genres to build an understanding of the many dimensions (e.g., philosophical, ethical, aesthetic) of human experience.	71
Apply a wide range of strategies to comprehend, interpret, evaluate, and appreciate texts. Draw on prior experience, interactions with other readers and writers, knowledge of word meaning and of other texts, word identification strategies, and understanding of textual features (e.g., sound-letter correspondence, sentence structure, context, graphics).	71, 77, 80, 83
Adjust the use of spoken, written, and visual language (e.g., conventions, style, vocabulary) to communicate effectively with a variety of audiences and for different purposes.	74, 83
Employ a wide range of strategies while writing, and use different writing process elements appropriately to communicate with different audiences for a variety of purposes.	71, 74, 77, 80, 83
Apply knowledge of language structure, language conventions (e.g., spelling and punctuation), media techniques, figurative language, and genre to create, critique, and discuss print and nonprint texts.	74, 77, 83
Conduct research on issues and interests by generating ideas and questions, and by posing problems. Gather, evaluate, and synthesize data from a variety of sources (e.g., print and nonprint texts, artifacts, people) to communicate discoveries in ways that suit the purpose and audience.	71
Use a variety of technological and informational resources (e.g., libraries, databases, computer networks, video) to gather and synthesize information and to create and communicate knowledge.	71, 83
Participate as knowledgeable, reflective, creative, and critical members of a variety of literacy communities.	74, 80, 83
Use spoken, written, and visual language to accomplish a purpose (e.g., for learning, enjoyment, persuasion, and the exchange of information).	74, 77, 80, 83

Introduction

An ancient Chinese proverb claims: "Tell me, I forget. Show me, I remember. Involve me, I understand." This timeless saying insinuates what all educators should know: Unless students are involved and actively engaged in learning, true learning rarely occurs.

The latest brain research reveals that both the right and left hemispheres of the brain should be engaged in the learning process. This is important because the hemispheres talk to one another over the corpus callosum, the structure that connects them. No strategies are better designed for this purpose than graphic organizers and visuals. Both of these strategies engage students' visual modality. More information goes into the brain visually than through any other modality. Therefore, it makes sense to take advantage of students' visual strengths to reinforce and make sense of learning.

How to Use This Book

The activities in this book cover the content areas and are designed using strategies that actively engage the brain. They are presented in the way the brain learns best, to make sure students get the most out of each lesson: focus activity, modeling, guided practice, check for understanding, independent practice, and closing. Go through each step to ensure that students will be fully engaged in the concept being taught and understand its purpose and meaning.

Each step-by-step activity provides one or more visual tools students can use to make important connections between related concepts, structure their thinking, organize ideas logically, and reinforce learning. Graphic organizers and visuals include extended cluster map, pie chart, coordinate grid, learning log, network tree, newspapers, double bar graph, geoboards, timeline, story analysis map, trading cards, bulletin board display, character chart, and more!

These brain-compatible activities are sure to engage and motivate every student's brain in your classroom! Watch your students change from passive to active learners as they process visual concepts into learning that is not only fun, but also remembered for a lifetime.

Put It Into Practice

Lecture and repetitive worksheets have long been the traditional way of delivering knowledge and reinforcing learning. While some higher-achieving students may engage in this type of learning, educators now know that actively engaging students' brains is not a luxury, but a necessity if students are truly to acquire and retain content, not only for tests, but for life.

The 1990s were dubbed the Decade of the Brain, because millions of dollars were spent on brain research. Educators today should know more about how students learn than ever before. Learning style theories that call for student engagement have been proposed for decades, as evidenced by research such as Howard Gardner's theory of multiple intelligences (1983), Bernice McCarthy's 4MAT Model (1990), and VAKT (visual, auditory, kinesthetic, tactile) learning styles theories.

I have identified 20 strategies that, according to brain research and learning style theory, appear to correlate with the way the brain learns best. I have observed hundreds of teachers—regular education, special education, and gifted. Regardless of the classification or grade level of the students, exemplary teachers consistently use these 20 strategies to deliver memorable classroom instruction and help their students understand and retain vast amounts of content.

These 20 brain-based instructional strategies include the following:

1. Brainstorming and Discussion

2. Drawing and Artwork

3. Field Trips

4. Games

5. Graphic Organizers, Semantic Maps, and Word Webs

6. Humor

7. Manipulatives, Experiments, Labs, and Models

8. Metaphors, Analogies, and Similes

9. Mnemonic Devices

10. Movement

11. Music, Rhythm, Rhyme, and Rap

12. Project-based and Problem-based Instruction

13. Reciprocal Teaching and Cooperative Learning

14. Role Plays, Drama, Pantomimes, Charades

15. Storytelling

16. Technology

17. Visualization and Guided Imagery

18. Visuals

19. Work Study and Apprenticeships

20. Writing and Journals

This book features Strategy 5: Graphic Organizers, Semantic Maps, and Word Webs, and Strategy 18: Visuals. Both of these strategies focus on integrating the visual and verbal elements of learning. Picture thinking, visual thinking, and visual/spatial learning is the phenomenon of thinking through visual processing. Since 90% of the brain's sensory input comes from visual sources, it stands to reason that the most powerful influence on learners' behavior is concrete, visual images. (Jensen, 1994) In addition, linking verbal and visual images increases students' ability to store and retrieve information. (Ogle, 2000)

Graphic organizers are visual representations of linear ideas that benefit both left and right hemispheres of the brain. They assist us in making sense of information, enable us to search for patterns, and provide an organized tool for making important conceptual connections. Graphic organizers, also known as word webs or semantic, mind, and concept maps, can be used to plan lessons or present information to students. Once familiar with the technique, students should be able to construct their own graphic organizers, reflecting their understanding of the concepts taught.

Because we live in a highly visual world, using visuals as a teaching strategy makes sense. Each day, students are overwhelmed with images from video games, computers, and television. Visual strategies capitalize specifically on the one modality that many students use consistently and have developed extensively—the visual modality. Types of visuals include overheads, maps, graphs, charts, and other concrete objects and artifacts that clarify learning. Since so much sensory input comes from visual sources, pictures, words, and learning-related artifacts around the classroom take on exaggerated importance in students' brains. Visuals such as these provide learning support and constant reinforcement.

These memorable strategies help students make sense of learning by focusing on the ways the brain learns best. Fully supported by the latest brain research, these strategies provide the tools you need to boost motivation, energy, and most important, the academic achievement of your students.

CHAPTER 1

Mathematics

Sports Mania: Pie Chart

Skills Objectives
Collect, organize, and communicate data.
Use percentages to express data.
Compare parts to a whole.

Materials
Pie Chart
reproducible

colored pencils or
markers

The ideal way to show numerical data is to use a graph or chart. A **Pie Chart** helps students present a visual overview of information when the total is known. Divided into sectors that represent percentages or fractions of the whole, a pie chart allows students to quickly compare different parts of the same whole.

1. Write on the board: *green, yellow, pink, blue, red*, and *other*. Read the name of each color aloud and ask students to raise a hand when they hear their favorite. Note that they may vote only once, and if their favorite color isn't listed they should vote for *other*.

2. Draw a pie chart on the board and divide it into ten equal sections. Explain that a pie chart is usually used to show fractions or percentages. Ask: *What percent does each section represent?* (10%) Point out that all the sections must add up to 100%.

3. Tell students that they are going to figure out what percentage of the class likes each color. Invite them to help you convert the survey results into percentages and fill in the chart.

4. Ask students to think of other types of information they could show on a pie chart (e.g., data represented as percentages or fractions). Give students a copy of the **Pie Chart reproducible (page 11)**, and write the Croft Elementary Team Sports data on the board.

Team Sports at Croft Elementary School	
Soccer	30%
Baseball	25%
Track	20%
Football	15%
Others	10%

Percentages and Degrees

To determine the portion of a circle needed to represent a certain percentage, multiply the percentage by 360 degrees (total number of degrees in a circle). For example: 50% is .50 x 360, or 180 degrees of the circle.

5. Draw another pie chart on the board and label it *Team Sports*. Divide it into ten equal sections. Ask students: *What is the most popular sport at Croft Elementary? How many sections of the pie chart should I label **soccer**?* (three sections) Label those sections *30%*. Ask volunteers how much of the chart represents baseball, track, and football, and label them with the correct percentages. Label the last section of the chart *other*, and explain that it stands for any other sports combined.

6. Instruct students to choose a topic for their own pie chart. As they are working, check for understanding. Be sure students use the same unit of measure for all the information, that they define what the whole stands for, and account for all of the parts within the whole. Students may draw additional lines on their chart to show more data or data in smaller increments (such as 5%).

7. Display students' finished charts and allow time for questions. Ask students if they can think of other ways to show the same data.

Extended Learning

- Divide the class into small groups. Have each group conduct a class survey on a topic such as favorite subjects or pets, and then show the data on a pie chart.

- If you have computer access, students can use the Circle Chart maker at Shodor Interactive: *www.shodor.org/interactivate/activities/CircleGraph*.

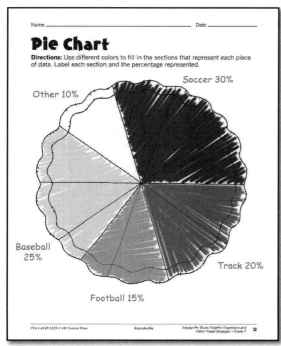

Pie Chart

Directions: Use different colors to fill in the sections that represent each piece of data. Label each section and the percentage represented.

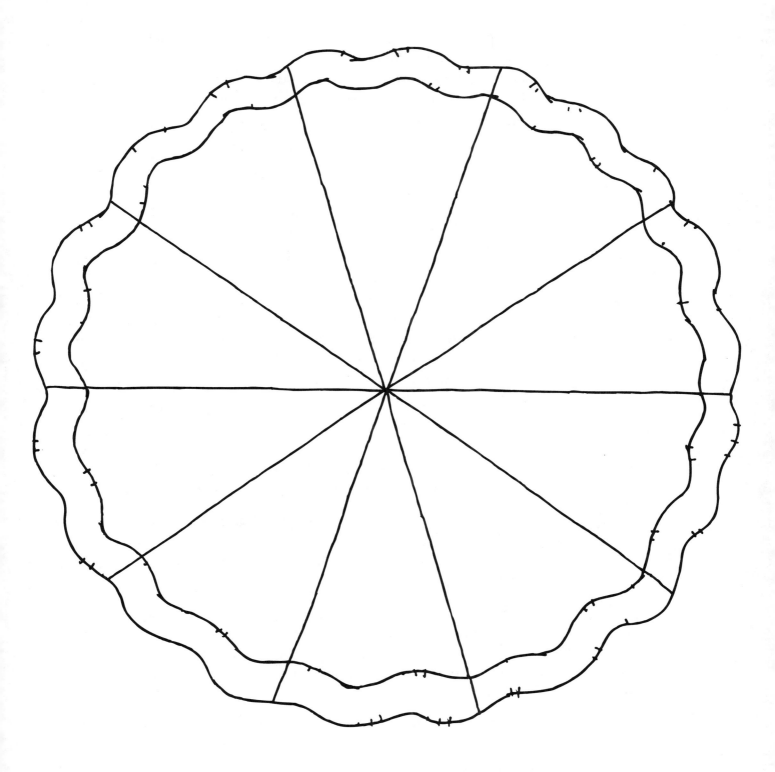

Plot the Points: Coordinate Grid

Materials

Plot the Points reproducible

tape measure

chalk

clipboards

Skills Objectives

Understand patterns and relationships.

Use representations such as graphs and grids.

Inquiry-based learning using props such as a life-sized **Coordinate Grid** helps students gain knowledge through physical activity. This can reinforce the important points of a lesson and increase retention of key points, particularly for the kinesthetic learner. By observing students during this activity, you'll also have an opportunity to assess their ability to follow directions.

1. Before you begin the lesson, locate an area, such as a sports court, where you can draw a large coordinate grid with chalk. The grid should be ten feet square. Label the first vertical line on the left Y (y-axis) and the first horizontal line X (x-axis). The vertical and horizontal lines should be one foot apart.

2. Tell students they will work with a life-sized grid, but first you will give a demonstration in the classroom. Explain that you are thinking of a desk in the room, and you want them to guess which one it is. Give students a clue, such as: *The first row of desks on my left, from front to back, is row Y. The desk I am thinking of is Y3.* Students should easily determine that you mean the third desk from the front.

3. Explain that the first row across, from your left to right, is row *X*. Ask students to find desk *X5*. They should choose the fifth desk from the left. Point out that they can find any desk in the room by using both *X* and *Y* row numbers. Ask a volunteer to find the desk at *X2, Y4*. Explain that *X2* and *Y4* are called *coordinates*.

4. Give students a copy of the **Plot the Points reproducible (page 14)**. Point out that the *Y* indicates vertical points (up and down), and the *X* indicates horizontal points (across). The straight lines that cross or intersect are called *axes*.

5. Give each student a clipboard for his or her reproducible, and then take the class outside to the chalk grid. Ask a volunteer to stand on the point at *X4, Y6*. Ask another student to stand on *X3, Y2*. Continue having volunteers stand at various points or move around the grid.

6. Tell students that the grid can also be used to measure distance between two points. The parallel lines are exactly one foot apart.

Have one student stand at *X3, Y4*. Have another student stand at *X3, Y6*. Ask a volunteer to determine the distance between these two points. *(two feet)*

7. Ask three volunteers to stand at random spots on the grid. Have students use their reproducible grids to plot each position. Repeat the activity several times, and allow students to call coordinates as well.

8. As an extra challenge, design simple pictures ahead of time that can be created with a set of coordinates. After calling the coordinates, invite students to plot the coordinates on their grids, connect the points, and guess the picture.

Extended Learning

- Set up a scavenger hunt in the classroom by hiding candy or other prizes in or under desks. Using the desks as points of reference, create a grid "treasure map" for students.

- Divide the class into seven groups. Have each group work together to identify these grid-related terms: *abscissa, axis, Cartesian coordinate system, ordinate, origin, plane, quadrant*. Then have groups present their findings to the class.

- Invite students to play games while mastering their understanding of the Cartesian coordinate system. Go to Shodor Interactive at: *www.shodor.org/interactivate/activities/SimpleCoordinates (or GeneralCoordinates)*.

Plot the Points

Directions: Use this grid to plot points, as directed by your teacher.

Number Please! Flowchart

Skills Objectives
Recognize and extend patterns.
Identify missing segments of patterns.
Understand number relationships.

Materials
Pattern Flowcharts reproducible

Pattern-based thinking is important at every level of math. To help develop this skill, encourage students to recognize simple number patterns, make predictions, recognize gaps in a number sequence, and determine how to extend a pattern. A **Flowchart** is generally used to show the developmental stages of a process and is easily customized to show mathematical progression in numbers and shapes, enabling students to look for patterns in numerical groupings.

1. Ask students to define the term *pattern*. Accept any answer that describes it as a series, sequence, or progression of numbers or shapes that is repeated, or that follows a predictable structured arrangement.

2. To demonstrate, choose a simple rhythmic pattern of claps and finger snaps such as: *clap three times, snap once, clap three times, snap once, clap three times.* Run through the pattern and ask students to predict what comes next and why. The answer should be *snap once.* Allow volunteers to create similar patterns and challenge the class to extend them.

3. Give students a copy of the **Pattern Flowcharts reproducible (page 17)**. Explain that they are going to use the flowcharts to help them look for numerical patterns. Draw a line of nine squares on the board. Fill in the first pattern from the following sample patterns. Write a question mark in the last box.

> **Sample Patterns**
> 1. Which number continues the pattern?
>   0, 5, 7, 12, 14, 19, 21, 26, . . . ?
>   (Pattern: +5 +2   Solution: 28)
> 2. Which number is incorrect?
>   10, 20, 15, 25, 20, 30, 40, 35, 30
>   (Pattern: +10 −5   Solution: 40 should be 25)
> 3. Which number is missing?
>   3, 9, 18, 54, 108, 324, ?, 1944, 3888
>   (Pattern: x3, x2   Solution: 648)

4. Ask students: *Can anyone see a pattern? What number do you think would extend the sequence? What operation can we use to get from zero to five? Should we add? How much?* Once a pattern becomes clear, suggest that students try repeating it to find the solution.

5. Write the second pattern on the board and have students write it in the first flowchart on their reproducible. Explain that one of the numbers in the pattern doesn't fit. Ask students to determine the incorrect number and replace it with a number that fits. Circulate around the classroom and give hints or suggestions when students seem stuck. Afterward, invite a volunteer to the board to show how he or she found the answer and write the rule.

6. Write the third pattern on the board, and point out that a number is missing. Allow time for students to figure out which number belongs in the sequence. Invite another volunteer to the board to show how he or she found the answer and write the rule.

7. Continue the activity by having students individually create their own patterns in the three remaining flowcharts. Have them exchange papers with a classmate to solve.

Extended Learning

- Bring in examples of geometric patterns in fabrics. Pass out art paper and colored pencils. Tell students to use shapes such as squares and triangles to create their own fabric patterns.

- Explain that there are many, varied patterns in nature and society. Have the class search for patterns in their everyday life and share their findings with the class.

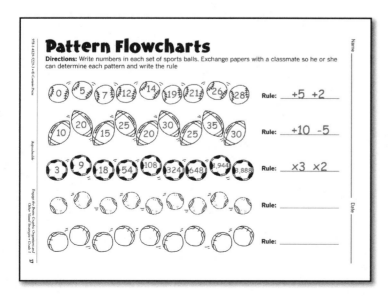

Name _____ Date _____

Pattern Flowcharts

Directions: Write numbers in each set of sports balls. Exchange papers with a classmate so he or she can determine each pattern and write the rule

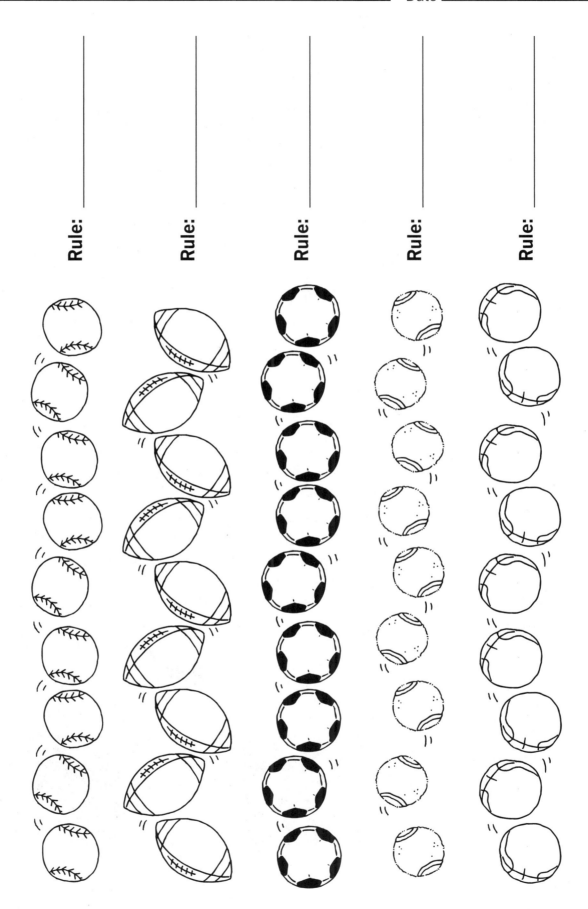

Rule: _____

Rule: _____

Rule: _____

Rule: _____

Rule: _____

Bits and Pieces: Manipulatives

Materials

Fraction Bars reproducible

Equivalent Fractions Table reproducible

10-piece fraction bars or lightweight poster board

rulers

scissors

Skills Objectives

Recognize equivalent fractions.

Understand that fractions are part of a whole.

Manipulatives enable teachers to use visual, auditory, tactile, and kinesthetic means to explore math concepts. For example, when comparing fractions, provide manipulatives, such as fraction bars, to help students visualize the concept. These handy classroom tools come in many shapes and sizes and can work with a variety of lessons. Commercially made models are convenient, but you can let students make their own sets using coins, buttons, craft sticks, or candy.

1. Give each student two ten-piece fraction bars, or have students make sets cut from 1" x 10" strips of poster board. Make sure they measure carefully so each bar is the same width and length.

2. Draw a ten-piece fraction bar on the board and have students follow along with their own bar. Ask: *How many sections are in this bar?* (ten) Ask a volunteer to write a fraction that represents one section. *(1/10)*

3. Erase two sections and ask: *How many sections are in the bar now?* (eight) Have another volunteer write a fraction that represents one section. *(1/8)*

4. Give students a copy of the **Fraction Bars reproducible (page 20)**. Tell them to use the bars to compare fractions. (They may also use them as a template to make their own sets of fraction bars.) Show students how to use the bars to compare fractions. For example,

ask: *Which is larger, 3/8 or 3/6?* Give them time to visually compare the two fraction bars on the reproducible. Continue asking questions until you are satisfied that students understand how to use the manipulatives.

5. Fraction bars are ideal for helping students understand the concept of equivalent fractions. Ask students to compare 1/2, 2/4, 3/6, 4/8, and 5/10. Ask students if these fractions are the same or different. Demonstrate that the last four fractions can be mathematically simplified to *1/2*. Then ask students: *How many ninths are equal to 1/3? (3/9)*

6. Give students a copy of the **Equivalent Fractions Table reproducible (page 21)**. Explain that the fractions in each row are equivalent. Allow time for students to use fraction bars to verify the fractions in each row. Monitor their progress.

7. Invite students to use their fraction bars and the Equivalent Fractions Table to write fraction problems for a classmate to solve. Have students store their fraction bars and Equivalent Fraction Table in a math folder for future reference or to use as study aids.

Extended Learning

- If students have access to a computer, guide them to the Arcytech Web site at *http://arcytech.org/java/fractions/fractions.html*. This excellent interactive site allows students to experiment with fractions, decimals, and percentages.

- Have students use their fraction bars to compare fractions in vertical rows of the Equivalent Fractions Table. For example: *Which is larger, 5/20 or 5/25?*

- Instruct students to create a percentages row on their Equivalent Fractions Table. Work with them on the first row to show that all of the fractions are equal to 100%.

Fraction Bars

Directions: Use these fraction bars to compare fractions and write fraction problems for classmates to solve.

$\frac{1}{1}$ $\frac{2}{2}$ $\frac{3}{3}$ $\frac{4}{4}$ $\frac{5}{5}$ $\frac{6}{6}$ $\frac{7}{7}$ $\frac{8}{8}$ $\frac{9}{9}$ $\frac{10}{10}$

Equivalent Fractions Table

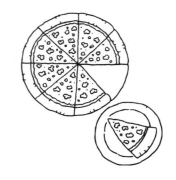

Directions: Find a fraction in the first column of the table. All of the fractions in that row are equal to it and to each other.

$\frac{1}{1}$	$\frac{2}{2}$	$\frac{3}{3}$	$\frac{4}{4}$	$\frac{5}{5}$	$\frac{6}{6}$	$\frac{7}{7}$	$\frac{8}{8}$	$\frac{9}{9}$	$\frac{10}{10}$
$\frac{1}{2}$	$\frac{2}{4}$	$\frac{3}{6}$	$\frac{4}{8}$	$\frac{5}{10}$	$\frac{6}{12}$	$\frac{7}{14}$	$\frac{8}{16}$	$\frac{9}{18}$	$\frac{10}{20}$
$\frac{1}{3}$	$\frac{2}{6}$	$\frac{3}{9}$	$\frac{4}{12}$	$\frac{5}{15}$	$\frac{6}{18}$	$\frac{7}{21}$	$\frac{8}{24}$	$\frac{9}{27}$	$\frac{10}{30}$
$\frac{1}{4}$	$\frac{2}{8}$	$\frac{3}{12}$	$\frac{4}{16}$	$\frac{5}{20}$	$\frac{6}{24}$	$\frac{7}{28}$	$\frac{8}{32}$	$\frac{9}{36}$	$\frac{10}{40}$
$\frac{1}{5}$	$\frac{2}{10}$	$\frac{3}{15}$	$\frac{4}{20}$	$\frac{5}{25}$	$\frac{6}{30}$	$\frac{7}{35}$	$\frac{8}{40}$	$\frac{9}{45}$	$\frac{10}{50}$
$\frac{1}{6}$	$\frac{2}{12}$	$\frac{3}{18}$	$\frac{4}{24}$	$\frac{5}{30}$	$\frac{6}{36}$	$\frac{7}{42}$	$\frac{8}{48}$	$\frac{9}{54}$	$\frac{10}{60}$
$\frac{1}{7}$	$\frac{2}{14}$	$\frac{3}{21}$	$\frac{4}{28}$	$\frac{5}{35}$	$\frac{6}{42}$	$\frac{7}{49}$	$\frac{8}{56}$	$\frac{9}{63}$	$\frac{10}{70}$
$\frac{1}{8}$	$\frac{2}{16}$	$\frac{3}{24}$	$\frac{4}{32}$	$\frac{5}{40}$	$\frac{6}{48}$	$\frac{7}{56}$	$\frac{8}{64}$	$\frac{9}{72}$	$\frac{10}{80}$
$\frac{1}{9}$	$\frac{2}{18}$	$\frac{3}{27}$	$\frac{4}{36}$	$\frac{5}{45}$	$\frac{6}{54}$	$\frac{7}{63}$	$\frac{8}{72}$	$\frac{9}{81}$	$\frac{10}{90}$
$\frac{1}{10}$	$\frac{2}{20}$	$\frac{3}{30}$	$\frac{4}{40}$	$\frac{5}{50}$	$\frac{6}{60}$	$\frac{7}{70}$	$\frac{8}{80}$	$\frac{9}{90}$	$\frac{10}{100}$

What Are the Odds? Tally Sheet

Materials

What Are the Odds? reproducible

coin

glass jar

jellybeans, 10 of each color (red, green, yellow, white, black)

Skills Objectives

Collect, organize, and interpret data.

Communicate data.

Predict probable outcomes.

Understanding probability and statistics is useful not only in math but across the curriculum. To build this knowledge, students must develop the skills needed to pose questions and assemble the data necessary to determine the answers. A **Tally Chart** is a simple and flexible organizer to help students collect, organize, and interpret data.

1. Explain to students that *probability* is chance or likelihood. Tell them to look out the window, and ask: *Do you think it will rain today?* If it is already raining, point out that the probability is 100%. If it is sunny and there isn't a cloud in the sky, the probability of rain is much lower. An  overcast sky could mean something in between. Ask students: *Who would benefit by knowing the probability of rain?* Possible answers might include *travelers, farmers,* and *weather forecasters.*

2. Show students a coin, and ask: *If I toss this coin 20 times, will it land on heads more often, tails more often, or is the probability the same?* Allow students to make their predictions and explain their reasons.

3. Draw a simple two-column tally chart on the board. Label one column *Heads* and the other *Tails.* Toss the coin 20 times. Record the results with tally marks. Repeat the experiment several times and average the results. Have volunteers take turns flipping the coin to see if that makes a difference in the outcome.

4. Explain that since the coin has two sides, the probability of it landing on heads is one chance out of two, or a ratio of 1:2. Note

that there is a very slight chance that the coin could land on its edge, but the probability is so low that it isn't worth considering.

5. Give students a copy of the **What Are the Odds? reproducible (page 24)**, and draw a sample chart on the board. Then count aloud the jellybeans of each color, and place them in the jar. In the chart's left column, write *red, green, yellow, white,* and *black*.

6. Ask students: *How many jellybeans are in the jar all together?* (50) *How many different colors and how many of each color are in the jar?* (ten each of five colors) Explain that if there are ten green jellybeans in a jar of 50, each time you draw a jellybean from the jar you have a ten in 50 chance that the jellybean will be green. Write *10:50* on the board. Ask students if there is a simpler way to write the ratio. *(1:5)*

7. Ask a volunteer to draw 20 jellybeans from the jar. On your tally chart, keep track of how many of each color the student draws. Total the number of each color in the *Total* column. Note that according to the ratio, four green jellybeans should have been picked. Check the actual number and discuss the results.

8. Divide the class into groups of three or four. Have each group design an experiment to test the probability of an event, and use their tally charts to record the results. Allow time for each group to present their experiment to the class.

Extended Learning

- Divide the class into several groups. Assign each group a topic such as weather forecasting, elections, or sporting events. Have each group research how and why probability is important for their topic, and then prepare a poster showing the results.

- Have students look up related vocabulary words such as *event, frequency, outcome, probability, random,* and *ratio.*

- Hold a Game Day and play games that involve the use of spinners or dice. Discuss the elements of chance that are part of each game.

- Invite students to explore probability at the Mrs. Glosser's Math Goodies™ interactive Web site: *www.mathgoodies.com/lessons/toc_vol6.html.*

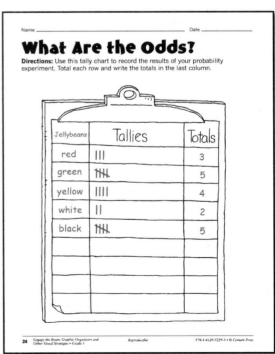

What Are the odds?

Directions: Use this tally chart to record the results of your probability experiment. Total each row and write the totals in the last column.

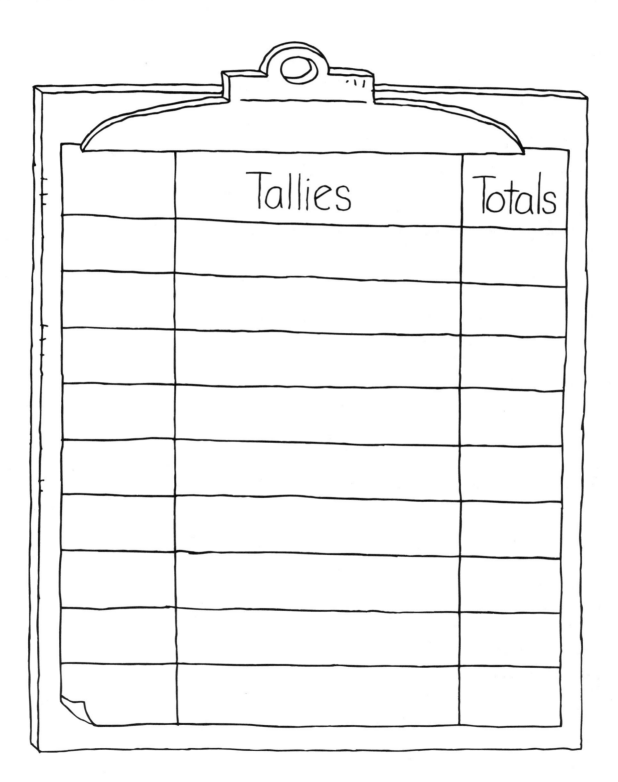

	Tallies	Totals

In My Own Words: Learning Log

Skills Objectives
Understand the journal writing process.
Communicate problem-solving strategies.

Materials
Learning Log reproducible

overhead projector and transparency

A math **Learning Log** encourages students to explore strategies for solving complicated math problems. This flexible tool enables students to focus on process, questions, feelings, and ideas, rather than simply coming up with the right answer. By writing or drawing in a log, students can express their thoughts and reason through problems. You may use prompts before giving students time to write, or simply make time at the end of a math lesson for a five-minute, free-flow log entry. A learning log can also be used as an excellent assessment tool.

1. Ask students to raise their hands if they keep a diary or journal. Ask volunteers to suggest things that might be included in a diary. For example: *things that happened that day; ideas for working through problems; plans and dreams for the future.* Tell students that writing about something can help them remember and understand it. In this activity, they will use a learning log, which acts like a math diary.

2. Give students a copy of the **Learning Log reproducible (page 27)**, and place a transparency of the reproducible on the overhead. Review the parts of the page with students. Point out the space for the date. Explain that sometimes you will give them a particular problem to consider; that is what goes in the space marked *Prompt*.

3. Tell students that a learning log is personal; entries will be different for each student. Point out that there are no right or wrong answers so students feel comfortable about writing exactly what they are thinking.

4. To demonstrate, give the class a sample word problem such as the following. Write the problem on the board and work through it with students. When you're finished, ask students to complete their Learning Log based on the work you did together.

Cleaning Up a Problem
Jonah and his friends helped to clear a vacant lot of trash. Each person picked up 20 pounds of trash. Jonah's older sister and her four friends picked up twice as much trash or 160 pounds in all. How many friends did Jonah have helping him?

Solution

If 160 pounds is twice the amount that Jonah and his friends picked up, then they must have gathered half of 160, or 80 pounds of trash. If Jonah and his friends each gathered 20 pounds of trash, then by dividing 80 total pounds by 20 we learn that there were 4 people on Jonah's team: Jonah and 3 friends. Jonah had 3 friends helping him.

5. Ask volunteers to share what they wrote. Discuss how creating such an entry can be useful as they study math over the school year. Remind students that entries can also serve as study aids for tests.

6. Distribute ten Learning Log pages to each student. Keep additional pages available for students to add to their logs. Invite students to keep pages together in a notebook, and use them whenever they think it might be helpful to write out their thoughts about solving particular math problems.

Extended Learning

Place a class Share Box where it is accessible to the class. Tell students that if while writing in their Learning Logs they come up with a question or idea to share with the class, they can jot it down on a piece of paper and put it in the Share Box. Once a week, evaluate the entries and read them aloud to the class.

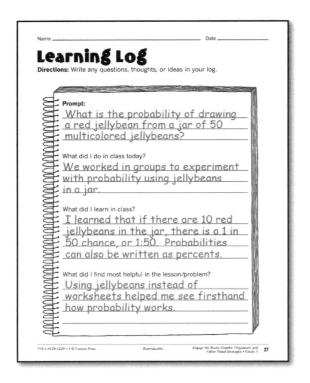

Learning Log

Directions: Write any questions, thoughts, or ideas in your log.

Prompt:

_____

_____

_____

_____

What did I do in class today?

_____

_____

_____

What did I learn in class?

_____

_____

_____

What did I find most helpful in the lesson/problem?

_____

_____

_____

_____

Get Onboard: Geoboards

Materials

All Kinds of Polygons reproducible

5 x 5 geoboards

rubber bands

Skills Objectives

Demonstrate an understanding of shapes.

Identify properties of a polygon.

Identify perpendicular and parallel lines.

A **Geoboard** is a manipulative designed to model such concepts as geometric shapes, perimeter, and area. A geoboard is a square board with raised pegs usually in a five-by-five pattern. Students place rubber bands over the pegs to create shapes of different sizes. Although commercial boards are generally the easiest to use, geoboards can be made with wood and nails or printed on paper and used with pencils. Interactive geoboards may also be found on the Internet.

Safety Note

When students use a geoboard for the first time, stress the importance of handling the rubber bands safely.

1. Begin the lesson by asking students to look around the classroom and point out as many different shapes as possible, including triangles, rectangles, squares, and circles. Ask students how the shape of something can affect its use.

2. Ask students if they have ever used a geoboard. Hold up a geoboard and point out the pegs. Demonstrate how to make a square by slipping a rubber band over the pegs. Ask students to name the shape. Have volunteers use geoboards to create other shapes, like pentagons, octagons, or other polygons.

3. Divide the class into pairs or groups, and distribute individual geoboards and rubber bands. Allow time for students to have an opportunity to use the geoboards to make shapes.

4. Distribute the **All Kinds of Polygons reproducible (page 30)**. Review the elements of each polygon. Ask questions such as: *How many sides does this shape have? Are all the sides equal? How many angles do you see?* Have students try to reproduce each shape on a geoboard. Allow plenty of time for students to experiment. Walk around the classroom and ask questions to check for understanding.

5. After students have had time to work with the geoboards, tell them to put away the reproducibles. Then direct them to make several shapes on their geoboard. Suggest a variety of shapes such as a three-sided shape, a polygon with two perpendicular sides, a

seven-sided figure, two congruent triangles, and so on. Invite volunteers to show their work to the class.

6. For more challenge, describe shapes for students to make on their geoboard. Then ask them to name each shape.

Extended Learning

- For interactive Internet geoboards, go to the National Council of Teachers of Mathematics (NCTM): Investigating the Concept of Triangle and Properties of Polygons at: *http://standards.nctm.org/ document/eexamples/chap4/4.2/index.htm.* Or go to the National Library of Virtual Manipulatives at: *http://nlvm.usu.edu/en/nav/ frames_asid_277_g_1_t_3.html.*

- Pair up students with partners. Have one student use different colored rubber bands to come up with a design on one half of the geoboard. Have his or her partner create the matching design "reflection" on the other half of the board.

- Have students come up with different ways to use the rubber bands to divide the geoboards in half, thirds, and quarters.

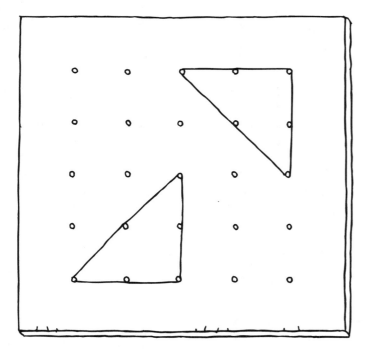
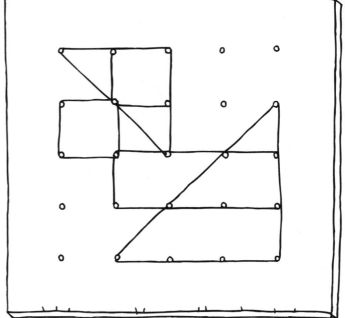

All Kinds of Polygons

Directions: Use your geoboard to create these shapes.

CHAPTER 2

Science

Tasty Atoms: Model

Skills Objectives

Understand that matter is made up of atoms.
Identify the parts of an atom.
Collect, communicate, and compare and contrast data.

Materials
Periodic Table
of Elements
reproducible

miniature
marshmallows

jellybeans in 2
different colors

canned icing

toothpicks

paper towels

overhead projector
and transparency

Using a **Model** is an ideal way to reach visual and kinesthetic learners by helping them visualize abstract concepts. A model does not have to be an exact representation as long as it creates an opportunity for discussion and so aids student understanding.

1. Show the class the jellybeans and marshmallows, and tell them that they will be using the sweets to make a model. Ask students: *Do you know what jellybeans are made of?* The answer will probably be *sugar*. Then ask: *What is sugar made of?* Explain that sugars are generally made up of the element carbon and water, and water is made up of the elements hydrogen and oxygen. But it doesn't end there!

2. Explain that elements are made up of tiny units called *atoms*. Atoms are the smallest unit of an element that still has the properties of that element. Ask if it is possible to break down an atom into even smaller parts. *(yes)*

3. Divide the class into pairs, and give each pair access to the materials. Tell students that they will use jellybeans and marshmallows to make a model showing the parts of an atom.

4. Draw a helium atom on the board. When you make the nucleus, draw circles for the two protons and two neutrons. Have volunteers name the parts of the atom, while you label them. *(nucleus, proton, neutron, electrons)*

5. Show students how to construct a model helium atom by sticking two red and two yellow jellybeans together with canned icing. Allow the nucleus to dry as you place toothpicks in two miniature marshmallows.

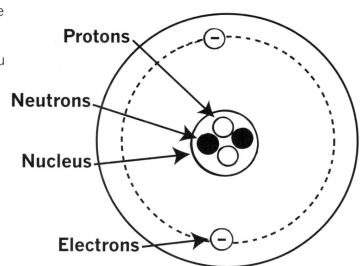

Explain that the marshmallows are electrons. Carefully insert the opposite end of each toothpick into the nucleus to complete your model.

6. Note that making a model of an atom is a good way to remember the different parts. Explain that in reality the relative sizes of the nucleus and electrons are quite different, and electrons do not circle the nucleus in tidy little orbits.

7. Distribute the simplified **Periodic Table of Elements reproducible (page 33)**. If possible, display a sample on an overhead and point to helium. Explain that the number in the box stands for how many protons are in the nucleus. The letter is the symbol for the element. Tell students that they may make a model of helium, lithium, or carbon.

8. Circulate around the classroom as students construct their models. Provide moist paper towels, as models may become a little sticky. Once the models are complete, discuss the definitions of *neutron, proton,* and *electron.*

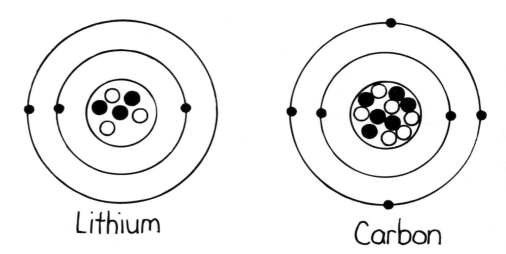

Lithium   Carbon

Extended Learning
- Have students draw their atom and include such information as the atomic number, atomic mass, symbol, and name of the element.

- Invite students to explore an interactive periodic table online at WebElements™: *www.webelements.com/webelements/index.html.*

Periodic Table of Elements

1 H																		2 He
3 Li	4 Be											5 B	6 C	7 N	8 O	9 F	10 Ne
11 Na	12 Mg												13 Al	14 Si	15 P	16 S	17 Cl	18 Ar
19 K	20 Ca	21 Sc	22 Ti	23 V	24 Cr	25 Mn	26 Fe	27 Co	28 Ni	29 Cu	30 Zn	31 Ga	32 Ge	33 As	34 Se	35 Br	36 Kr
37 Rb	38 Sr	39 Y	40 Zr	41 Nb	42 Mo	43 Tc	44 Ru	45 Rh	46 Pd	47 Ag	48 Cd	49 In	50 Sn	51 Sb	52 Te	53 I	54 Xe
55 Cs	56 Ba		72 Hf	73 Ta	74 W	75 Re	76 Os	77 Ir	78 Pt	79 Au	80 Hg	81 Tl	82 Pb	83 Bi	84 Po	85 At	86 Rn
87 Fr	88 Ra		104 Rf	105 Db	106 Sg	107 Bh	108 Hs	109 Mt	110 Ds	111 Rg	112 Uub	113 Uut	114 Uuq	115 Uup	116 Uuh	117 Uus	118 Uuo

57 La	58 Ce	59 Pr	60 Nd	61 Pm	62 Sm	63 Eu	64 Gd	65 Tb	66 Dy	67 Ho	68 Er	69 Tm	70 Yb	71 Lu
89 Ac	90 Th	91 Pa	92 U	93 Np	94 Pu	95 Am	96 Cm	97 Bk	98 Cf	99 Es	100 Fm	101 Md	102 No	103 Lr

Sliding Along: Demonstration and Project Planner

Materials

Science Project Planner reproducible

thumbtack

wide rubber band

3" of 2" x 4" wood

various surfaces (sandpaper, tile, wood, glass)

ruler

Skills Objectives

Use prior knowledge.

Evaluate and organize data.

A classroom **Demonstration** doesn't have to be complex to have an impact on learning. Through visualization and group discussion, a demonstration can support the inquiry process and help increase student retention. To make sure the demonstration runs smoothly, keep it as simple as possible and complete a **Project Planner**, explain each step as you progress, ask students for comments and predictions, and address any safety concerns before you begin.

1. Tell students that you will perform a simple demonstration to show how friction affects movement. Instruct students to rub their hands together quickly. Ask: *Do your hands feel any different? How?* (They feel warmer.) Ask if anyone knows why their hands warm up when they rub them together. The answer is *friction*. Explain that friction is the resistance between surfaces as they move over each another. The movement results in heat.

2. Now that you have set the stage, demonstrate that some materials create more friction than others. Use a thumbtack to attach a rubber band to a three-inch block of wood. Place the wood block on a flat, smooth surface, and have a volunteer measure and record the length of the unstretched rubber band.

3. Continue the demonstration by pulling gently on the rubber band until the block begins to slide. Measure and record the length

of the stretched rubber band. Ask students to predict what will happen if you try to slide the block over a rough surface.

4. Repeat Step 3 on a variety of surfaces. Note that the block slides more easily on smoother surfaces. Have students compare the recorded lengths of the rubber band. Explain that the rougher the surface the more force is needed to overcome the friction. Instead of moving the block, the applied force stretches the rubber band. When enough force is applied, the block moves.

5. Have students predict what would happen if you put oil on the rough surface. Ask them to explain their thinking.

6. Encourage students to discuss their observations. Ask if anyone has a suggestion for improving the demonstration.

7. Distribute the **Science Project Planner reproducible (page 36)**. Divide the class into groups of three or four students. Instruct each group to use the reproducible to plan a demonstration of friction in any form they wish.

8. When the planners are complete, allow time for each group to perform their demonstration and share their Project Planners with the class.

Extended Learning

- Pair your class with a class that is at least two years younger. Divide your class into four groups, and have each group design a science demonstration to present to the younger class. Working with younger children can increase the confidence and self-esteem of older students and improve communication skills.

- Invite a guest expert to do a demonstration in the classroom and discuss the benefits of a career in science.

- If you have access to a video camera, have students produce a video science demonstration. Play it for the class or put it on the school Web site.

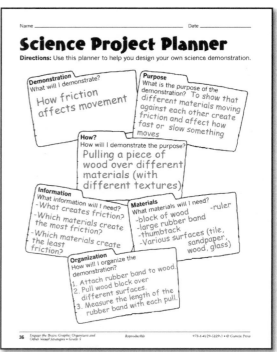

Science Project Planner

Directions: Use this planner to help you design your own science demonstration.

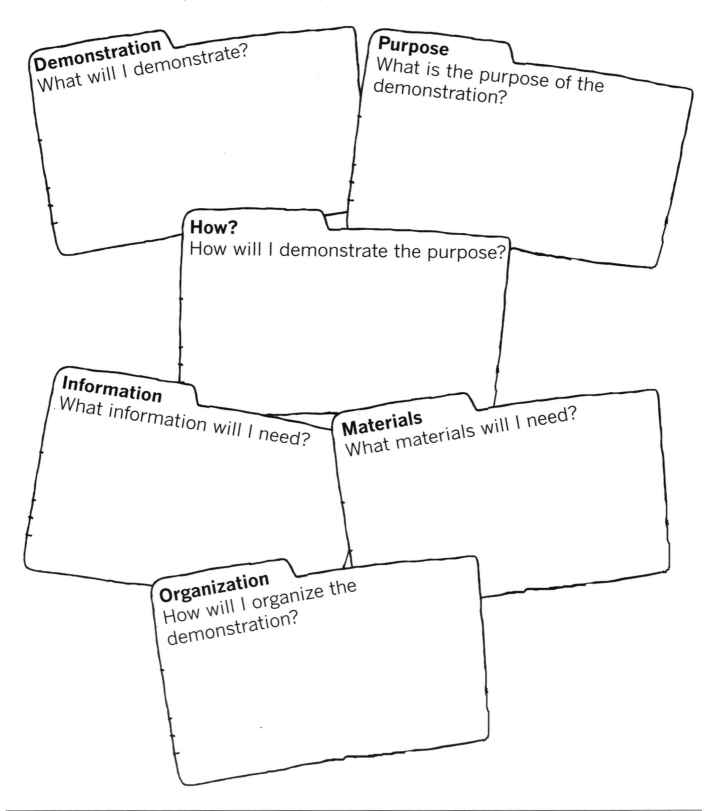

Demonstration
What will I demonstrate?

Purpose
What is the purpose of the demonstration?

How?
How will I demonstrate the purpose?

Information
What information will I need?

Materials
What materials will I need?

Organization
How will I organize the demonstration?

Statistically Speaking: Double Bar Graph

Skills Objectives
Represent and interpret data in a bar graph.
Recognize patterns.

Materials
Double Bar Graph
reproducible

outdoor
thermometer

Double Bar Graphs present facts and statistics in a visual form that makes the information easier to compare. This helps students organize and interpret contrasting data and draw conclusions about the information.

1. Tell students that you are going to conduct a class survey about favorite seasons. Write *Spring, Summer, Fall,* and *Winter* on the board. Ask students to raise their hand for their favorite season. Record the number of responses in each column.

2. Draw a bar graph on the board, with the numbers *1–20* along the vertical axis and the names of the seasons along the horizontal axis. Illustrate how the information from the survey is shown as bars on the graph.

3. Repeat the survey. This time, divide the class into two groups, A and B. Survey Group A and Group B separately. Redraw the bar graph on the board showing the results for both groups for each season. Explain that this is a double bar graph.

4. State that showing the results of a survey is one way a bar graph may be used. Share the following data about average temperatures in U.S. cities in January and July. Explain that you will be using a double bar graph to track two sets of data and compare the average temperatures of the hottest and coldest months.

Average Temperatures		
City	**January**	**July**
Anchorage, AK	16°F	58°F
Boston, MA	29°F	74°F
Honolulu, HI	73°F	81°F
Los Angeles, CA	57°F	69°F
Phoenix, AZ	54°F	93°F
New York, NY	32°F	77°F
Washington, DC	34°F	79°F

5. Draw the axes on the board. Label the horizontal axis *Cities* and the vertical axis *Temperature*. Ask students: *Which city has the warmest temperature in January? Which city has the least temperature difference between January and July?* The answer to both questions is *Honolulu*.

6. Point out that there is a difference of about 77 degrees between the coldest and warmest temperatures on the graph. Ask students: *What would be the best scale to use for our graph?* Guide students to select increments of ten degrees. Note that there are also short lines on the vertical axis. Ask: *How many degrees does each of the short lines represent?* (two degrees)

7. Write the names of the cities along the horizontal axis. Then ask volunteers to draw each pair of bars over the cities. Once the graph is complete, ask students questions such as: *Which city is hottest in July? Which two cities have the greatest temperature difference between January and July? What is the average temperature in Los Angeles over the period from January to July?*

8. Distribute the **Double Bar Graph reproducible (page 39)**. Show students the outdoor thermometer. Explain that they will take temperature readings outside of the classroom in the morning and afternoon for seven days. Ask what steps they should take to be certain the data is as correct as possible. Answers may include: *Take the readings in the same place each time. Take the readings at the same time every day.*

9. Once students have gathered the information, direct the class to use their reproducible to make a double bar graph to display the data. Review the graphs and note any errors such as incorrect labels or inconsistent scales.

Extended Learning

- Explain that bar graphs are a very common tool for showing science data. Ask students to bring in examples from magazines and newspapers.

- Inform students that line plots are another kind of graph used to monitor changes in temperature. Have students show the temperature data they gathered on a line plot. Ask students to explain which graph was easier to use and why.

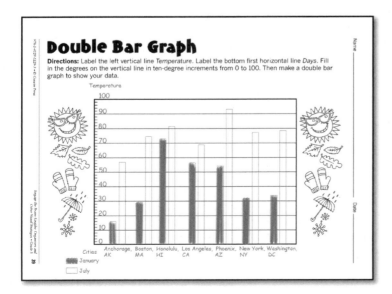

Double Bar Graph

Directions: Label the left vertical line *Temperature*. Label the bottom first horizontal line *Days*. Fill in the degrees on the vertical line in ten-degree increments from 0 to 100. Then make a double bar graph to show your data.

Spectacular Systems: Extended Cluster Map

Materials

Major Body Systems reproducible

Extended Cluster Map reproducible

colored pencils

research materials such as encyclopedias, nonfiction books about the body, and the Internet

Skills Objectives

Discover relationship between topics or ideas.

Organize data in a graphic organizer.

An **Extended Cluster Map** can display large amounts of data in a clear, visual way. It's an excellent tool for grouping together the elements of a unit that have similar, dependent, and sometimes overlapping features. Individual units can then be grouped to illustrate how they relate to each other as parts of a whole. In this way, the extended cluster map is ideal for showing the major systems of the human body.

1. Ask students to brainstorm functions that the body performs automatically. Write the answers on the board. Answers may include *breathe*, *heart beats*, *sweat*, *heal*, *grow*, *digest food*, and *feel pain*. Now ask for some things the body does that you can control. Answers may include: *eat*, *talk*, *read*, and *walk*. Explain that all of these things are controlled by one or more major systems in the body.

2. Distribute the **Major Body Systems reproducible (page 42)**. Tell students that these systems are what make the body function. They work together as a team. For example, if you want to catch a ball, your brain communicates your thoughts to the body through the nervous system. The skeletal and muscular systems work together to support your body and make it move. You see the ball with your eyes, which are part of the sensory system.

3. Review each system and discuss its main functions. Allow plenty of time for questions. Ask students to think of some other ways that the systems work together, such as while eating or sleeping.

4. Distribute the **Extended Cluster Map reproducible (page 43)**. Draw a cluster map on the board. Write *Body Systems* in the center circle. In the outer circles write the names of the major systems from the reproducible. Tell students to work along on the reproducible using a different colored pencil for each system. Point out the lines extending from each outer circle. These are for functions of each system. Ask students to brainstorm resources they can use to find the answers.

5. Allow students to work with a partner to research the functions using encyclopedias, library books, and online sources. Partners can each take responsibility for certain systems and then share the information.

Extended Learning

- Divide the class into 11 groups. Assign each group a body system and have them create a cluster map naming the major organs of that system and their functions.

- Divide the class into groups of four or five students. Have them work together to create an *Owner's Manual* for a healthy body.

- If students have access to a computer, they can find information about body systems from the American Medical Association: Atlas of the Body: *www.ama-assn.org/ama/pub/ category/7140.html*.

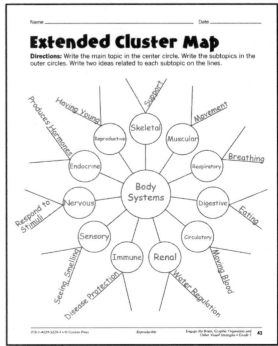

Major Body Systems

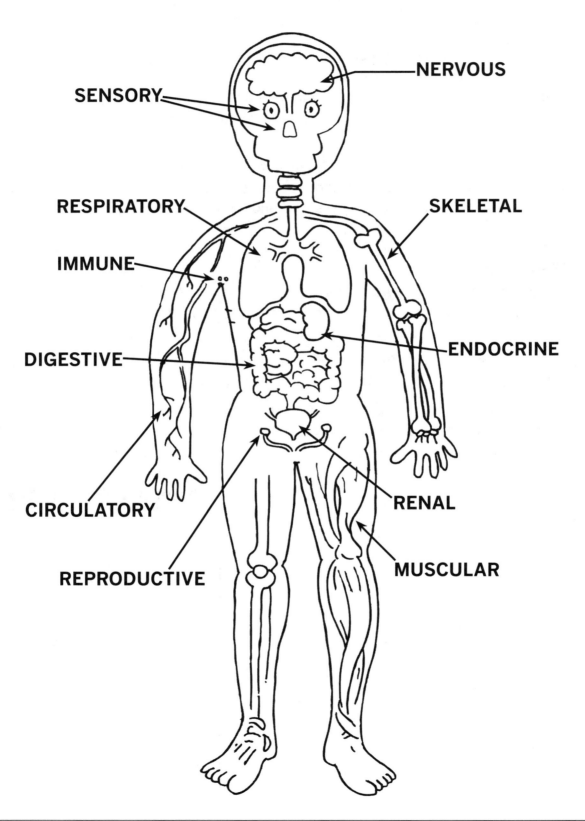

NERVOUS

SENSORY

RESPIRATORY

SKELETAL

IMMUNE

DIGESTIVE

ENDOCRINE

CIRCULATORY

RENAL

REPRODUCTIVE

MUSCULAR

Name _____ Date _____

Extended Cluster Map

Directions: Write the main topic in the center circle. Write the subtopics in the
outer circles. Write two ideas related to each subtopic on the lines.

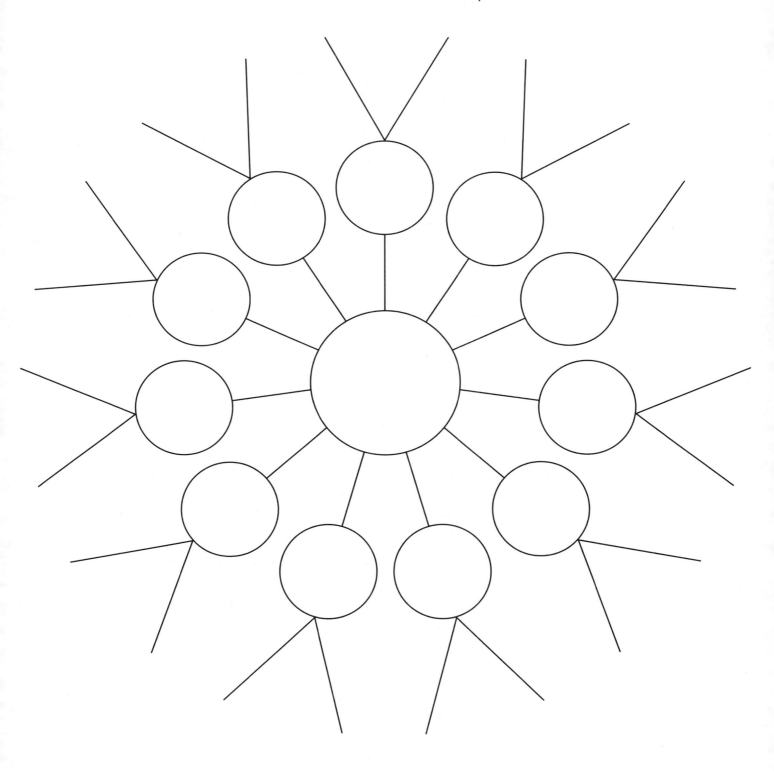

A Close Examination: Venn Diagram

<table>
<tr><td>

Materials

Gills and Lungs reproducible

A Close Examination reproducible

book

notebook

</td></tr>
</table>

Skills Objectives

Understand structure and function in living systems.

Compare and contrast data.

Analyze information.

A **Venn Diagram** is a graphic organizer that can help students easily record, compare, and contrast information. In a life science unit, it can be helpful for comparing the physical characteristics or behavior of animals. Insights gathered by using a Venn diagram can lead to a deeper understanding of the living world.

1. Introduce the concept of "compare and contrast" by holding up two similar objects such as a book and a notebook. Ask: *How are they alike? How are they different?* Similarities might include: *They are both made from paper. They both have pages and covers.* Differences might include: *Notebook pages are blank. You write in a notebook. Books pages have printing. You don't write in books.*

2. Tell students that they will closely examine one aspect of animals—how they breathe. Explain that some animals breathe through gills (fish) and others breathe with lungs (mammals). Students will use a Venn diagram to compare and contrast gills and lungs.

3. Give each student two copies of the **A Close Examination reproducible (page 47)**. Ask students what they already know about how our lungs work, and then, how gills work. Write suggestions on the board.

4. Give students a copy of the **Gills and Lungs reproducible (page 46)**. Have volunteers read the information aloud as the class follows along. Allow time for questions to be sure students understand the information.

5. Draw a Venn diagram on the board and model using it for students. Label one circle *Gills* and the other circle *Lungs*. Label the overlapping section *Both*. Say: *In the center section, where the circles overlap, we will write how gills and lungs are alike. Who can tell me a characteristic they share?* Answers may include: *They are both used for breathing. They both contain arterioles.*

6. Instruct students to write contrasting characteristics in the outer circles. For example, under *Gills* write: *Water enters the mouth and leaves through gill slits.* Under *Lungs* write: *Air enters and leaves through the nose and mouth.*

7. Check that students understand how to record similar and contrasting information on the Venn diagram. Then have them use their blank Venn diagram to compare and contrast other structures, such as a plant cells and human cells or wings and fins. Students can work individually or in pairs. You may want to assign topics or make sure each pair is working on a different type of structure.

8. Once students complete their Venn diagrams, ask volunteers to share their work with the class. Bind all the work together in a class science book for student reference.

Extended Learning

- Have students use a Venn diagram to compare two animals from a similar environment, such as a polar bear and caribou from a polar environment.

- Introduce students to the term *parallel evolution*. Divide the class into groups of three or four, and have each group find an example of plants or animals that illustrate parallel evolution, such as the green tree python and emerald tree boa. Then have them create a Venn diagram to compare the animals.

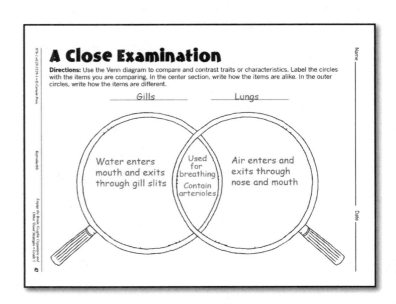

Gills and Lungs

Fish and mammals process air and oxygen differently. Fish have gills so that they can take oxygen from the water. Mammals have lungs so that they can take oxygen from the air.

Gills

Most fish take water in through the mouth. When the mouth closes it forces the water across the gills and out the gill slits. The water exits a different way than it came in. Water contains much less oxygen than air, so gills have to be better than lungs at drawing out oxygen. To do this, the blood in the gills moves in the opposite direction to the water flow. (In fish, blood is pumped in only one direction by a two-chambered heart.) Gills contain paired filaments attached to a sturdy but hollow gill arch. The arches have arteries inside them. These arteries divide into smaller arterioles inside the filaments. Each filament has tiny folds called *lamellae* that increase surface area. Tiny capillaries from the arterioles carry blood to the inner surface of the lamellae. Oxygen then spreads into the blood through this thin membrane.

Lungs

Most land animals, including humans, breathe in air through their nose and mouth. Lungs then draw in oxygen from the air. As the animal inhales, the diaphragm and muscles between the ribs contract and expand the chest cavity. Air flows in through the bronchi and inflates the lungs. The air then flows through smaller and smaller bronchioles until it reaches the alveoli. Oxygen spreads into the blood through a thin membrane in the alveoli. (In mammals, blood is pumped in two directions by a four-chambered heart.) Oxygen is exchanged for carbon dioxide, which is breathed out the same way it came in. It is exhaled through the nose and mouth.

A Close Examination

Directions: Use the Venn diagram to compare and contrast traits or characteristics. Label the circles with the items you are comparing. In the center section, write how the items are alike. In the outer circles, write how the items are different.

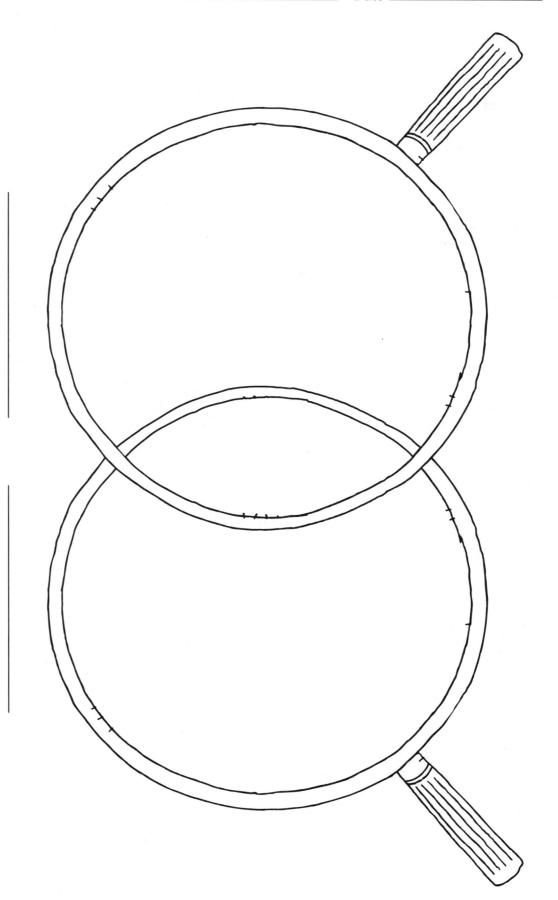

Science Discoveries: Word Wall and Word Map

Skills Objectives

Use context clues and prior knowledge to find word meaning.
Understand chronological order or the sequence of events.
Understand a repetitive cycle.

Materials

Earth's Water Cycle reproducible

Word Map reproducible

overhead projector and transparency

A **Word Wall** is an effective visual learning tool for students. Among its many advantages are its access and flexibility. Words can be attached using Velcro or pushpins, so students can easily change or update them. For science vocabulary, terms may be listed in logical categories, such as physical science, life science, and earth science. Another great visual tool is a **Word Map**. This kind of chart allows students to study important terms by definition, description, and other details such as origin or appearance.

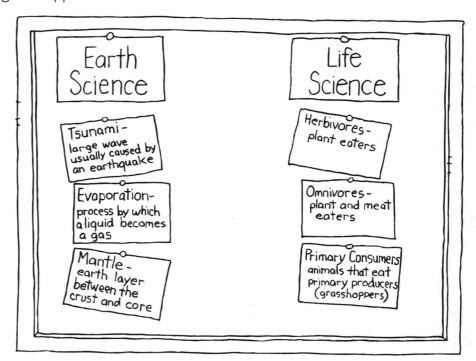

1. Tell students that you will work together as a class to build a class science word wall of important terms and definitions. Explain that it will be a reference they can use throughout the year. Everyone will contribute words and definitions during different units of study.

2. Demonstrate by making a sample word wall together. Give students a copy of the **Earth's Water Cycle** and **Word Map reproducibles (pages 50–51)**. Review the water cycle with the class. Then place a transparency of the word map on the overhead.

3. Select one vocabulary word, such as *precipitation*, and write it in the top box of the word map. Ask students: *What is the definition of **precipitation**?* (any form of water that falls to earth's surface) Write the answer in the *Definition* box.

Sample Vocabulary Words

condensation	hydrologic cycle
precipitation	vapor
evaporation	climate
liquifaction	air pressure

4. Have a volunteer give a physical description of precipitation, for example: *snow, rain, hail, sleet*. Write the response in the *Description* box. Note that it would also be acceptable to draw a picture.

5. The *Details* box is for any additional points or clarification. Explain that this can be anything to help describe the word, including a picture. One response for *precipitation* might be: *a major part of the water cycle*.

6. Instruct students to choose a term from the Earth's Water Cycle reproducible and fill in their own word map. When they are done, post the papers on a bulletin board. Have students read the terms and choose the top ten for the word wall. Explain that words may be added or changed as you progress through different units.

Extended Learning

- Word walls are most effective when referred to often. After a word wall has been up for about a week, play "mystery word" by removing one term and asking students to guess which one is missing. If they cannot guess the term, give a hint by reading the definition.

- Ask students to bring in pictures or graphs from newspapers and magazines to illustrate the words on the word wall.

- Play the game of Hangman with the class using words from the word wall.

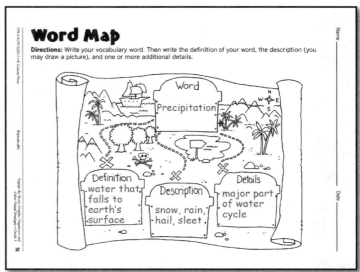

Earth's Water Cycle

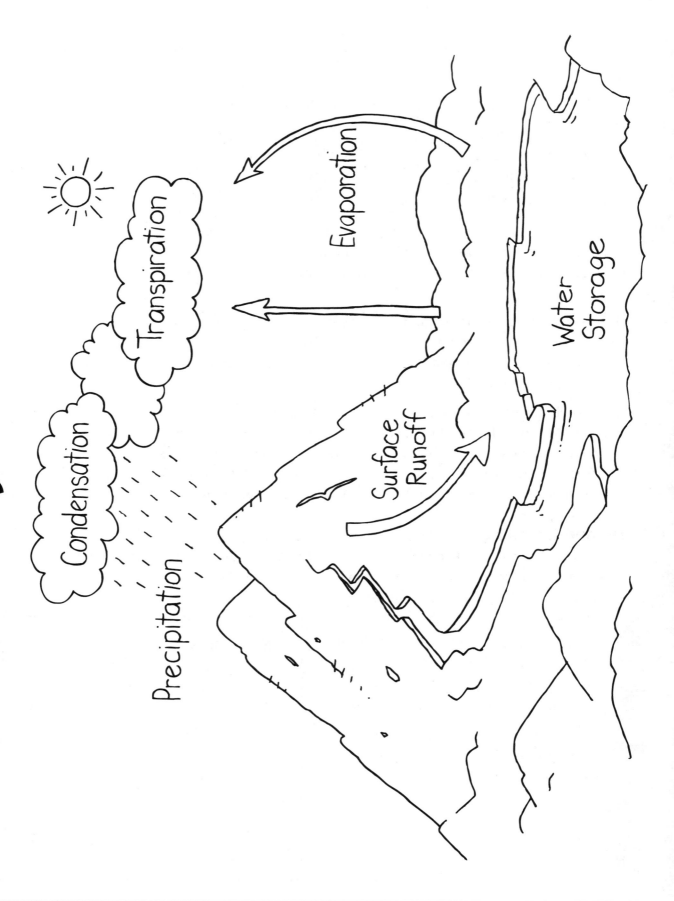

Name _____ Date _____

Word Map

Directions: Write your vocabulary word. Then write the definition of your word, the description (you may draw a picture), and one or more additional details.

Our Town: KWL Chart

Materials

KWL Chart reproducible

sample travel brochures

Skills Objectives

Read and write for a purpose.
Use prior knowledge.
Identify relevant details and key information.
Collect and communicate information.

Students are naturally curious about their place in the world and their community. Acquiring knowledge about a topic such as the local community usually leads to further questions. The **KWL Chart** is a good tool for helping students to learn by drawing on previous knowledge, anticipating what will come, targeting particular information, and summarizing what they learned. The chart can also be used as a study guide or a source for an outline for a written report or oral presentation.

1. Allow students to browse a collection of travel brochures. Point out that the information appears in short, appealing phrases and paragraphs. Ask students to find any interesting, entertaining, or attention-grabbing words or phrases. Explain that brochures serve a variety of purposes. They might be aimed at traveling families interested in historical landmarks or attractions; business people interested in hotels and meeting facilities; or new residents interested in job opportunities, housing, and schools.

2. Divide the class into three groups. Explain that each group will research information for a brochure about their community. Assign each a target audience, such as travelers, business people, or new residents. Note that although each brochure has a special focus, all brochures should include information on services and entertainment.

3. Give students a copy of the **KWL Chart reproducible (page 54)**, and draw a simple, three-column KWL chart on the board. Explain that the K stands for what students already *know*. The W stands for what they *want* to know. The L stands for what they *learn*.

4. Ask students to help you fill in the KWL chart on the board. Ask them for general information that should go in each brochure by brainstorming a list of local sights and attractions. Ask: *If you had friends coming to visit, what would you want them to see and do?* Write their suggestions in the K column.

5. Have students suggest things they would like to know about their community. Write their suggestions in the W column. For example: *Who is the mayor? Are there any pet-friendly hotels? Who founded the town and when?*

6. Tell the class they will have several days to do their research. Have students work in groups to complete the K and W columns on their charts. Suggest that students use books, magazines, and online sources to search for the answers to their questions, and record them in the L column of their chart. Point out that personal interviews can also be a great resource. As students work, monitor them to make sure that they are on the right track.

7. Once research is complete, invite each group to create a travel brochure for their assigned target audience. Encourage them to use pictures, photos, and drawings to make their brochures interesting and fun.

8. When brochures are finished, invite each group to present its brochure to the class. Invite the class to vote on the most interesting, creative, and appealing brochure. During a follow-up discussion, ask students how the KWL Chart helped them organize their information.

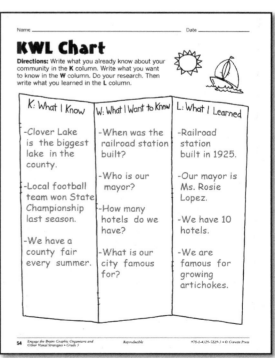

Name _____ Date _____

KWL Chart

Directions: Write what you already know about your community in the **K** column. Write what you want to know in the **W** column. Do your research. Then write what you learned in the **L** column.

K: What I Know	W: What I Want to Know	L: What I Learned
-Clover Lake is the biggest lake in the county.	-When was the railroad station built?	-Railroad station built in 1925.
-Local football team won State Championship last season.	-Who is our mayor? -How many hotels do we have?	-Our mayor is Ms. Rosie Lopez. -We have 10 hotels.
-We have a county fair every summer.	-What is our city famous for?	-We are famous for growing artichokes.

54 *Engage the Brain: Graphic Organizers and Other Visual Strategies • Grade 3*   Reproducible   978-1-4129-5229-3 • © Corwin Press

KWL Chart

Directions: Write what you already know about your community in the **K** column. Write what you want to know in the **W** column. Do your research. Then write what you learned in the **L** column.

K: What I Know   W: What I Want to Know   L: What I Learned

A Little Bit of History: Newspaper and 5W Chart

Skills Objectives

Read and write for a purpose.

Use prior knowledge.

Conduct an interview.

Identify relevant details and key information.

Newspapers are important instructional tools in any classroom. They generally offer a concise, tightly organized story with clear emphasis on facts. Using a **5W Chart** along with a newspaper encourages students to listen carefully as they note important facts and details. These kinds of charts help students focus on the **W**ho, **W**hen, **W**here, **W**hat, and **W**hy of a story.

1. Initiate a class discussion by stating that most Americans have ancestors from other countries. Ask students to share from where their families originated. Write the list of nations on the board. Explain that although America has a unique culture, it includes echoes of the cultures of immigrants who helped build it.

2. Brainstorm with the class some everyday things that originated in other countries. Examples include foods such as spaghetti, clothing such as the beret, and games such as soccer.

3. Give students a copy of the **5W Chart reproducible (page 57)**. Point out that the five *W*s stand for *who, what, when, where,* and *why.* Explain that you will read aloud a short newspaper article. As you read, students should listen for the answers to those five questions.

4. When you're done reading, tell students they will write a newspaper article about a person whose family immigrated to America. They may interview their own relatives or those of a friend or neighbor.

5. Explain that much of the information in the article should come from their interview. Ask students to brainstorm some questions they might ask about their subject's family origin, history, customs, and traditions. Write the questions on the board. For example:
   • *Where and when were you born?*
   • *When did you immigrate to the United States?*
   • *Where did your family settle, and why?*
   • *What brought your family to the United States?*
   • *What opportunities did your family find here?*

6. Give students the opportunity to take notes and copy questions. Instruct them to use the 5W Chart during their interview as well. Give students at least a week to conduct their interviews and complete their charts.

7. Have students turn in their 5W Charts before they write their articles. Check that they are filled in correctly and show an understanding of the process. Return the charts and instruct students to complete their articles.

8. Compile students' articles into a class "historical" newspaper. Invite your writers to read their articles aloud or share them in small groups. Make a list of all the countries from which people originated and plot them on a world map display.

Extended Learning
   • Have students draw a picture or take a photograph of the interviewee to accompany their article.

   • Have students read a selection of letters to the editor in a newspaper. Then invite them to write a letter to the editor, as a class, commenting on the article they read.

5W Chart

Directions: Fill in the chart as you interview your subject. Write the headline. Then write *who* the article is about, *what* happened, *when* it happened, *where* it happened, and *why* it happened.

Headline

Who?

What?

When?

Where?

Why?

Roots of a Revolution: Network Tree

Materials

Network Tree reproducible

overhead projector and transparency

Skills Objectives

Use prior knowledge.

Classify information.

Understand historical relationships.

Draw conclusions from research.

Network Trees are hierarchical graphic organizers. They can help students sort or classify information, and show how elements are related. The network tree is an excellent tool for helping students get a clear overview of complex topics, such as the American Revolution, and organize data from multiple sources to reflect superordinate and subordinate elements.

1. Ask students if they have ever had an argument with a friend or family member. If so, tell them to consider how it developed. Explain that disagreements are rarely caused by one thing, but usually a combination of causes.

2. Relate your discussion to the American Revolution by explaining that the war didn't suddenly happen overnight. There were social factors and events that led up to the conflict. Several reasons led the nation to war, but you will examine only one—The Boston Tea Party. Ask volunteers to tell what they know about that event, and write their answers on the board.

3. Give students a copy of the **Network Tree reproducible (page 60)**, and place a transparency of the reproducible on the overhead. Write *American Revolution* in the bottom box. Write *Boston Tea Party* in one of the connecting boxes. Point out the three lines connected to each box. Explain that these are for details about the event. The British East India Company was given unfair advantage to sell tea in the colonies without import tax. Write *Tea Act* on the first line.

4. Then ask: *Who can tell me what the colonists did?* Answers might include: *The Sons of Liberty dressed up as Mohawk Indians, boarded the ships, and dumped the tea in the harbor.* Write *Colonists dumped tea* on the next line. Add that the British closed Boston Harbor and passed unfair laws such as the Intolerable Acts. Write *Intolerable Acts* on the last line.

5. Divide the class into small groups, and have each group research events that led to the American Revolution. Tell them to fill in their network trees with facts from their research.

6. Invite students to share their results. Then have each group take turns contributing to a larger network tree on a Revolutionary War-themed bulletin board. Make sure all main ideas and details are represented on the finished bulletin board.

Extended Learning

- The Boston Tea Party took place on Thursday, December 16, 1773. Many nations celebrate events from their political history. Have the class design a celebration to commemorate the day, including a traditional meal, games, and other activities.

- Have students create network trees for each of the following: French and Indian War, The Stamp Act, The Intolerable Acts, The Boston Massacre.

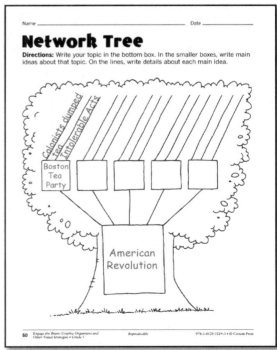

Network Tree

Directions: Write your topic in the bottom box. In the smaller boxes, write main ideas about that topic. On the lines, write details about each main idea.

Patriots and Loyalists: T-Chart

Skills Objectives
Use prior knowledge.
Compare and contrast information.
Evaluate and communicate information.

Materials
Comparing Points reproducible

research materials such as encyclopedias, nonfiction books about the Revolutionary War, and the Internet

A **T-Chart** enables students to list information about two elements, and then visually compare, contrast, and clarify the material. Topics may be examined in a variety of ways, such as: pros and cons, advantages and disadvantages, causes and effects, problems and solutions, facts and opinions, or before and after.

1. Tell students that you are going to make a list of some of the most famous people of the Revolutionary War. Ask for suggestions and write them on the board, such as: *George Washington, Molly Pitcher, Nathan Hale, Benjamin Franklin, Paul Revere.* Tell students that these were all patriots. Then ask: *Can you think of any loyalists, or people who were in favor of the British?* Someone may mention Benedict Arnold, though he wasn't a true loyalist.

2. Inform the class that not every colonist wanted to fight for independence. Estimates are that up to one-fifth of colonists were loyalists. Write the following names on the board: *Bernardus Lagrange, William Franklin* (son of Benjamin Franklin), *John Singleton Copley,* and *Quakers.*

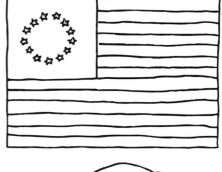

3. Give students a copy of the **Comparing Points reproducible (page 63)**. Tell students to title one column *Loyalist* and the other column *Patriot.* Then provide time for students to conduct research to come up with at least four points to support each side of the conflict. Suggest encyclopedias, trade books, and the Internet. One of many excellent Web sites is Colonial Williamsburg: Loyalty or Liberty? at: *http://www.history.org/History/teaching/revolution/loyalty. html.*

4. When students are finished, invite volunteers to share some of their ideas. Draw a T-chart on the board and write suggested points in each column. Then ask the class to decide which arguments are more convincing. Ask: *Would you have been a patriot or a loyalist? Why?*

5. Divide the class into four groups. Assign each group a loyalist and a patriot. Instruct them to create a poster

about each person. Display completed posters on a bulletin board.

Following are some notable names from the Revolutionary War:

- Abigail Adams
- John Adams
- Samuel Adams
- John André
- Benedict Arnold
- Crispus Attucks
- Lord Charles Cornwallis
- John Dickinson
- Benjamin Franklin
- King George III
- Nathaneal Greene
- Nathan Hale
- John Hancock
- Patrick Henry
- Richard Henry Lee
- General William Howe
- Thomas Jefferson
- Cybil Ludington
- Thomas Paine
- Molly Pitcher
- William Prescott
- Casmir Pulaski
- Paul Revere
- Betsy Ross
- Benjamin Rush
- Deborah Sampson
- Mercy Otis Warren
- George Washington
- Martha Washington
- Phyllis Wheatley

Extended Learning

- Have student pairs act out mock interviews with important figures of the American Revolution, such as Paul Revere, George Washington, Benedict Arnold, or John Hancock.

- Instruct students to use a T-chart to compare the commanding generals at Yorktown: George Washington and Lord Charles Cornwallis.

- Invite student groups to research the meanings of the following famous phrases from the Revolutionary War. Have them present their findings to the class.

    "The shot heard around the world"—The Story of Lexington and Concord

    "Give me liberty or give me death"—Patrick Henry

    "I regret that I have but one life to give for my country"—Nathan Hale

    "I have not yet begun to fight"—John Paul Jones

    "We must all hang together or we shall all hang separately"—The signing of the Declaration of Independence

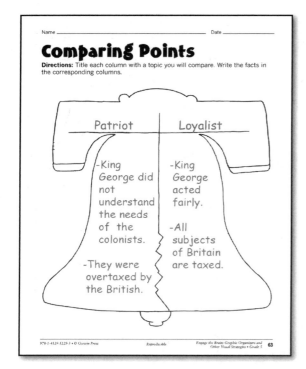

Comparing Points

Directions: Title each column with a topic you will compare. Write the facts in the corresponding columns.

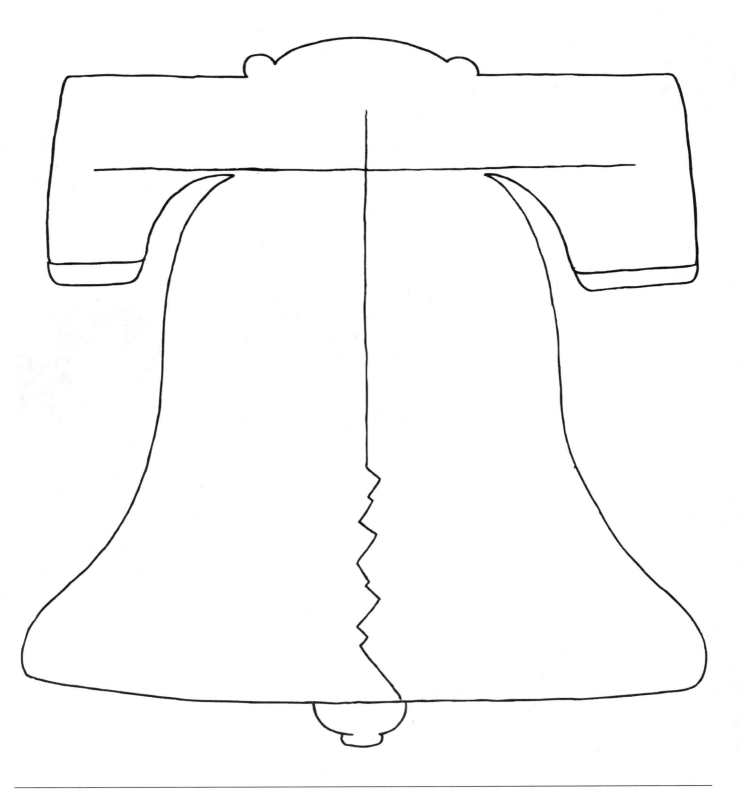

How a Bill Becomes a Law: Chain of Events Map

Materials

From Bill to Law:
Senate reproducible

Chain of Events Map
reproducible

overhead projector
and transparency

Skills Objectives

Recognize cause-and-effect relationships.
Understand chronological order or sequence.

A **Chain of Events Map** is a tool that allows students to show information in steps or stages, specifically to describe a sequence of events. This organizer guides students to visualize how one action or event leads to the next and, finally, to the outcome.

1. Begin the lesson by demonstrating the concept of a chain of events. Tell students to imagine that they are planting a tomato garden: *First, you prepare the soil. Then, you plant the seeds. Next, you water the seeds every day. Finally, the plants sprout.* Ask students what happens next. Answers might include: *The plant grows larger. It blooms and produces tomatoes.* Point out the logical progression of steps from beginning to end.

2. Give students one copy of the **From Bill to Law: Senate reproducible (page 66)** and two copies of the **Chain of Events Map reproducible (page 67)**. Ask a volunteer to read aloud "How a Bill Becomes a Law" while the rest of the class follows along.

3. Place a transparency of the Chain of Events Map on the overhead. Tell students to review "How a Bill Becomes a Law," and choose the most important steps to write in their first Chain of Events Map. Model how to fill in the first couple of steps on the transparency, or fill in the first and last step. The first step should be: *Senator introduces the bill.* The last step should be: *President signs the bill into law.*

4. Before they begin, make sure students understand that each

event must lead logically to the next. Allow them to discuss which steps belong in the other boxes, and in what order.

5. Note that the process of a bill becoming law is different in the House of Representatives than it is in the Senate. Allow access to the Internet or arrange a trip to the library so students can conduct research about that process. Invite them to complete their second Chain of Events Map about the House of Representatives.

6. When the assignment is complete, initiate a class discuss by comparing the two maps. Prompt students with questions such as: *Why do you think the process is different in the Senate than it is in the House of Representatives? Why do both chambers have to approve a bill before it can be sent to the President? Do you agree with the process? Why or why not?*

Extended Learning

Ask students to perform a vocabulary word search through newspapers and magazines for the terms *legislation, revision, amendment, debate, quorum, filibuster, compromise,* and *veto.* Invite them to share their findings with the class.

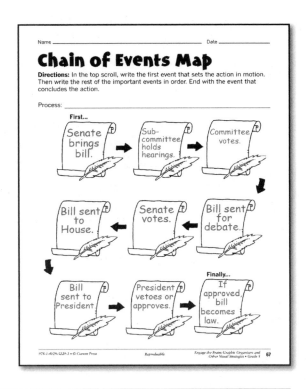

From Bill to Law: Senate

How a Bill Becomes a Law

When a Senator introduces a bill in the Senate, the bill is assigned a number and copies of it are made. The bill is then sent to committee and placed on the calendar. At that point, a bill can be assigned to a subcommittee who may hold hearings and recommend changes. The findings are reported to the full committee and a vote is taken.

If the bill is approved, the committee prepares a report explaining why they favor the bill. Committee members who oppose a bill sometimes write a dissenting opinion as well. The report goes back to the whole chamber and is placed on the calendar for debate.

In the Senate, debate is usually unlimited. Members can speak as long as they want. Finally, they vote on the bill. If the bill is approved, it goes to the House of Representatives. If either chamber of Congress (the Senate or House) does not pass the bill, the bill dies. If they both pass the bill, then the bill goes to the President.

If the President doesn't like the bill, he or she might veto it. If the President vetoes the bill, it goes back to Congress with a list of reasons for the veto. However, if the President approves of the bill, he or she signs it into law.

Chain of Events Map

Directions: In the top scroll, write the first event that sets the action in motion. Then write the rest of the important events in order. End with the event that concludes the action.

Process: _____

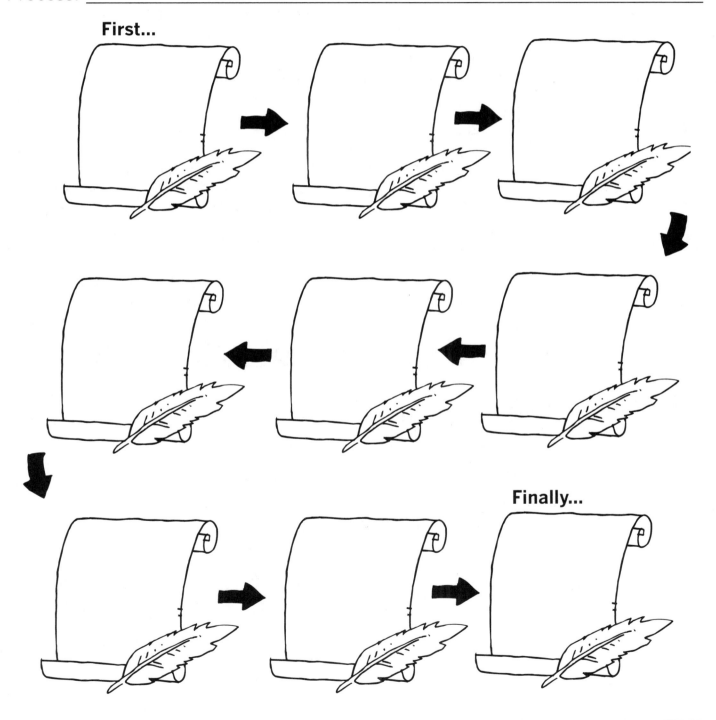

Reproducible   *Engage the Brain: Graphic Organizers and Other Visual Strategies • Grade 5*   **67**

Good Citizenship: Concept Wheel

Skills Objectives

Use prior knowledge.

Identify a main theme.

Understand relationships between ideas.

A **Concept Wheel** allows students to present concepts visually in a related group. This graphic organizer is often used as a language arts tool, but it may also be used for brainstorming ideas or to display related elements of a central topic.

1. Invite students to reflect on how much independence they had in first grade. Ask: *Have your privileges changed as you have grown older? What are you able to do now that you could not do before?*

2. Explain that as we grow up, we get more freedom to make our own decisions. Ask students what else they get more of as they grow older. Guide them to the idea of *responsibility*. Ask for examples such as: *You can go to a friend's house, but you have to be home on time. You get to stay alone in the house, but you have to care for a younger sibling. You get to go shopping, but you have to earn your spending money.*

3. Explain that adults have the same combination of independence and responsibility. For example, if you want the privilege of driving a car, you have to agree to follow traffic laws. Point out that being an American citizen works the same way. A citizen has many privileges, but also some important duties and responsibilities.

4. Give students a copy of the **Concept Wheel reproducible (page 70)**. Draw a copy of the wheel on the board, and write *Responsibilities of U.S. Citizens* in the center. Encourage the class to brainstorm what they believe are some duties and responsibilities of United States citizenship. Write their answers in the outer sections of the wheel. Answers may include: *vote; obey the law; defend the country; serve jury duty; stay informed; respect the rights of others; respect public property.*

5. Initiate a class discussion on why each of these duties and responsibilities are important. Ask students: *Why should a citizen be informed? What does that mean? Why does it matter if you vote?* Note that our legal system guarantees a person the right to a trial by a jury of his or her peers. Ask: *How does that relate to a citizen's duty to serve on a jury when called?*

6. At the conclusion of the discussion, give students time to fill in their concept wheels. Divide the class into small groups or pairs to debate which duties and responsibilities they feel are most important for U.S. citizens.

7. When students are finished, invite each group to share which duties they included in their concept wheel. Invite the whole class to debate which duties are most important and why.

Extended Learning

- Ask the class: *What are your responsibilities as students?* Answers may include: *do homework; pay attention in class; respect school property.* Have them complete a concept wheel to reflect the responsibilities of students.

- Have students write a story about a day with no laws. *What would the world be like? Would it be more dangerous? What might happen?*

- Show the class a copy of the original Bill of Rights. Point out the right of free speech. Ask students: *What responsibilities come with the right to free speech?* Answers may include: *speak honestly; be fair; speak respectfully about others.* Write the following quote by Chief Justice Oliver Wendell Holmes on the board: *The most stringent protection of free speech would not protect a man in falsely shouting "Fire!" in a theatre and causing a panic.* Ask students what he meant by this statement and how it applies to the responsibility of a citizen.

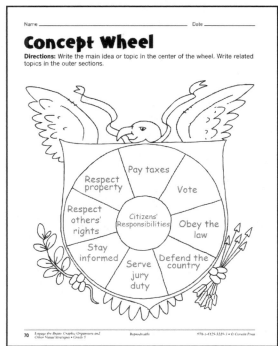

Concept Wheel

Directions: Write the main idea or topic in the center of the wheel. Write related topics in the outer sections.

CHAPTER 4

Language Arts

Path of a Lifetime: Timeline

Skills Objectives
Obtain information from multiple sources.
Isolate relevant details and key information.
Visualize key moments in chronological order.

Materials
Path of a Lifetime
reproducible

Timelines may be utilized in a variety of ways. For nonfiction, a timeline is a straightforward means to represent events in chronological sequence. For fiction, it enables students to grasp relationships within a storyline, highlight important events in a character's life, or place a character in the proper historical context. Understanding time frame provides an in-depth look into a character's behavior.

1. Draw a simple timeline on the board. Tell students that you would like to create a visual representation of a day in class. For example, ask: *How and when do we start our day? We start at 8:15 with attendance.* Write students' suggestions on the board until the timeline is complete.

2. Inform students that they will create a timeline about a person of historical importance based on independent reading. But first, you will make a timeline together. You may use a nonfiction or historical fiction book of your choice, or use the sample below about the life of Helen Keller.

3. Give students a copy of the **Path of a Lifetime reproducible (page 73)**, and draw another timeline on the board. Explain that the first step in making a timeline is to determine the endpoints. Ask students where you should start and end the timeline.

4. Begin the timeline with the birth of Helen Keller and end it with her death. Ask students to define the term *chronological order*. For example: *Putting events in order from the earliest to the most recent date.* Enter each date above the timeline and write the description below the timeline.

1880: Helen born in Alabama.
1882: Illness leaves her blind, deaf, and unable to speak.
1886: Annie Sullivan becomes Helen's teacher.

1890: Helen speaks using the Tadoma method.
1894: Helen and Anne move to New York City.
1904: Helen graduates from Radcliffe College.
1915: Helen founds Helen Keller International.
1960: Helen's book, *Light in My Darkness*, is published.
1964: Helen awarded the Presidential Medal of Freedom.
1968: Helen dies 26 days before her 88th birthday.

5. Once students understand how to create a timeline, ask them to make their own timeline using the reproducible. It will be based on a biography they have read or been assigned. They may focus on a single chapter or cover the entire book. Remind students to give their timeline an appropriate title and to write dates along the left side of the path and corresponding events on the right.

6. When students are finished, initiate a discussion about biographies. Ask questions such as: *What are some of the major elements of a biography? Why are biographies important? What can you learn from a biography? What is the difference between a biography and an autobiography?* Have students share the titles of their favorite biographies and autobiographies. Make a class list for future reference.

Extended Learning

- Note that it is the responsibility of the author to check facts for accuracy. Have students create a list of possible resources that an author can use to get information, such as other books, family members, and letters. Ask students to consider what to do if they find conflicting information in their research.

- Have students create an autobiographical timeline with pictures and illustrations.

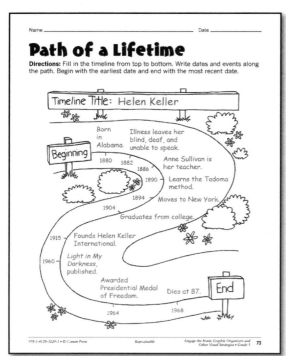

Path of a Lifetime

Directions: Fill in the timeline from top to bottom. Write dates and events along the path. Begin with the earliest date and end with the most recent date.

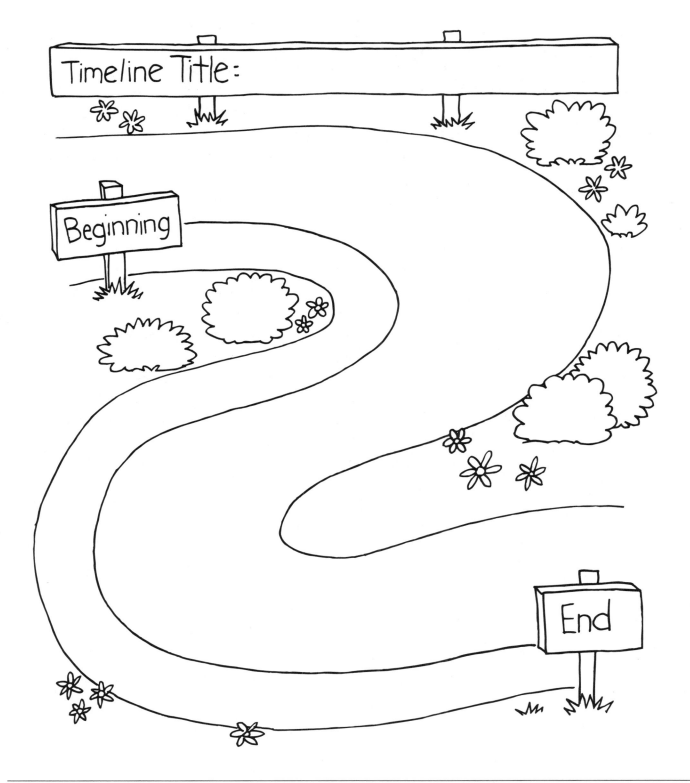

Visual Poetry: Cluster Map

Materials

Visualize It reproducible

overhead projector and transparency

thesauruses

chart paper

Skills Objectives

Use vivid word choices to support the main idea.
Apply poetic form.
Understand parts of speech.

Visual poetry, such as shape poetry and concrete poetry, is an excellent tool for developing sensory awareness. Writing visual poetry allows students to express their experiences and observations through creative language and word placement. A **Cluster Map** enables students to find the most precise, vivid words and create the desired image.

1. Draw a simple flower on the board, and invite volunteers to suggest adjectives to describe it. Encourage them to use all their senses. Write the words around your drawing. For example: *pretty, fragrant, striking, velvety, sweet, silky, pure, fresh, sleek, glossy, colorful.* Now use the words to create the outline of a flower.

2. Explain that visual poetry is a form that uses the placement of words as part of the poem. Note that word placement is either in the shape of the object or reflects some element of the object about which the poem is written.

3. Give students a copy of the **Visualize It reproducible (page 76)**, and place a transparency of the reproducible on the overhead. Point out the sun. Have students brainstorm words that relate to the sun and write them in the outer circles or "planets." Tell them they may use adjectives, nouns, and verbs. For example: *hot, ball, sizzle, fiery, golden, crimson, fierce, blaze, scorch, burning, blistering, warm, gentle, cozy, welcoming, orb, globe, sphere.*

4. Share the following poem using words students brainstormed.

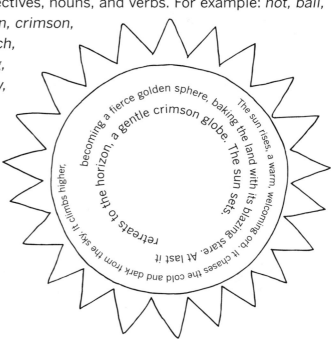

5. Provide students with thesauruses and invite them to complete their own cluster map. They can use their words to write about the sun, the solar system, the planets, or anything pertaining to the universe. While they are working, check that students understand how to use a thesaurus correctly and how to record words on the map.

6. Ask volunteers to read aloud their poems to the class or in small groups. While students are reading, list all the vivid, interesting words they used on chart paper for future reference. Display students' finished work around the classroom.

Extended Learning

- If you have computer access, find samples of poetry at PBS. org: Poetic Forms and Examples: *www.pbs.org/newshour/extra/ features/jan-june00/poetryboxformexamples.html.* Divide the class into groups, and have each group learn about a different form of poetry. Invite each group to share what they learned with the class, including an original example.

- If possible, help students to publish their poetry in the school newspaper or newsletter.

- Share examples of concrete poetry with students, such as "Letter Slot" by John Updike and "Concrete Cat" by Dorthi Charles.

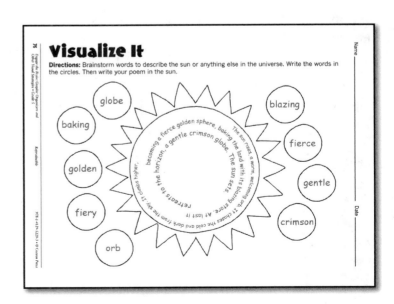

visualize It

Directions: Brainstorm words to describe the sun or anything else in the universe. Write the words in the circles. Then write your poem in the sun.

Engage the Brain: Graphic Organizers and Other Visual Strategies • Grade 5   *Reproducible*   978-1-4129-5229-3 • © Corwin Press

Figuratively Speaking: Word Map

Skills Objectives

Use background knowledge to predict meaning.
Employ context clues to interpret meaning.
Understand the usage and meaning of figurative language.
Identify the meanings of idioms.

Materials

Illustrious Idioms reproducible

overhead projector and transparency

Familiarity with figurative language enables students to better understand texts that contain such devices as idioms, similes, metaphors, and personification. A **Word Map** is a graphic organizer that helps students build that familiarity. In this activity, students gather a collection of clues that help them use language in context. Complementing the word map with a physical activity, such as charades, makes the experience more memorable and exciting!

1. Ask students if they know what it means when someone says: *You can't pull the wool over my eyes* or *I've run out of steam*. If they don't know, explain the meaning of each phrase. Point out that no one is actually trying to pull wool over their eyes. it means that they're trying to fool you. Running out of steam means they are worn out and tired, but not that they produce any actual steam.

2. Explain that these phrases are known as *idioms*. An idiom is an expression whose meaning is not related to the exact words used. Review the following samples with students.

Idioms

- A little bird told me
- He's an accident waiting to happen
- At each other's throats
- Back to the drawing board
- It left a bad taste in my mouth
- Don't beat around the bush
- She talks behind his back
- Bend over backwards
- Clutching at straws
- Every cloud has a silver lining
- I'm in over my head
- Go fly a kite
- Shooting the breeze
- Take the bull by the horns
- Put the cart before horse

3. Give students a copy of the **Illustrious Idioms reproducible (page 79)**, and place a transparency of the reproducible on the overhead. Write an idiom, such as *A knight in shining armor*, in the *Idiom* box. Ask students for suggestions as you fill in the other boxes.

Ask a volunteer to guess the meaning of the idiom. For example: *Someone who helps when you are in a difficult situation*. Write the answer in the *Meaning* box.

4. Have a volunteer suggest an original sentence incorporating the idiom to write in the *Sentence* box. For example: *He showed up like a knight in shining armor and helped me fix my car*. In the *Picture* box, invite a volunteer to come to the board and draw something to illustrate the meaning of the idiom.

5. Direct students to choose an idiom, and then develop their word map independently or with a partner. As students work, make sure they understand how to fill in the reproducible correctly.

6. For a fun follow-up exercise, organize the class into two teams for a game of Charades! Invite student pairs to choose idioms to act out for classmates to guess.

Extended Learning
- For a comprehensive list of creative idioms and their origins, access the IdiomSite at: *www.idiomsite.com.*

- Use a word map to generate a writing assignment. Encourage students to write a paragraph or two inspired by their idiom.

- Invite students to make up their own idioms and explain them to the class.

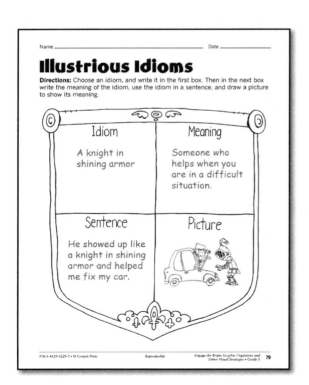

Illustrious Idioms

Directions: Choose an idiom, and write it in the first box. Then in the next box write the meaning of the idiom, use the idiom in a sentence, and draw a picture to show its meaning.

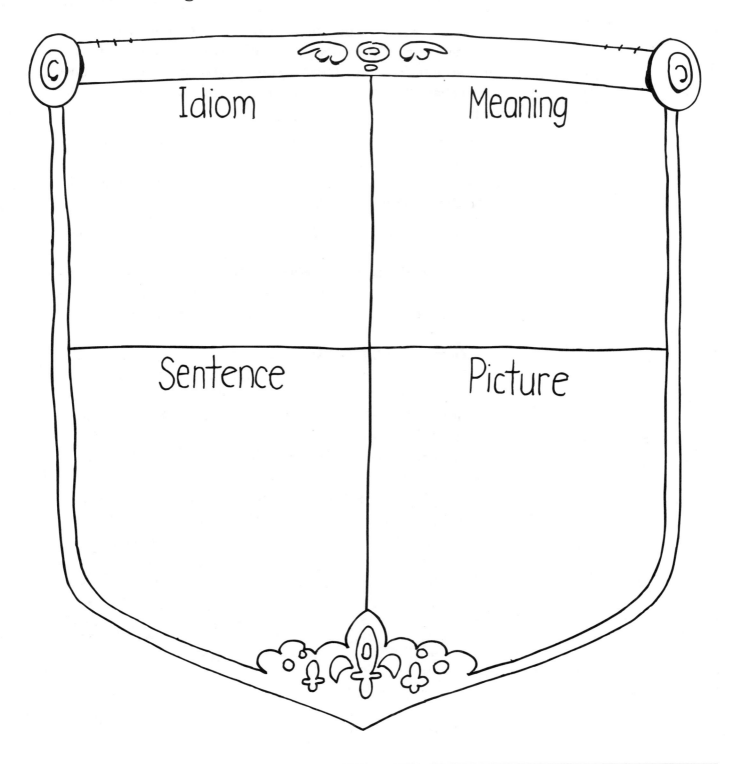

Developing Character: Character Chart

Materials

Character Chart reproducible

Skills Objectives

Recognize character development.

Isolate relevant details and key information.

Strong characters are one of the most important elements of a well-written story. A student writer can better understand the central character's goals and motivations by making a **Character Chart** for their protagonist. The chart clarifies point of view and becomes a template for the writer to revisit as the story develops. This enables students to create a character who is well-rounded and dynamic rather than flat and static.

1. Ask students to think of a book character they liked. Have them share the reasons why they find the character appealing and interesting. Then ask students to share their thoughts about a character they did not like.

2. Inform students that they will write a short story, and the first element they will work on is characterization. Give them a copy of the **Character Chart reproducible (page 82)**. Discuss some of the traits that their main character might have. Then share the following character elements to help students brainstorm ideas.

> **Elements of Character**
>
> **Physical Description:** What does the character look, dress, walk, and talk like?
>
> **Background:** What are the character's talents, skills, family life, and past experiences?
>
> **Personality:** Is the character shy, outgoing, loud, nervous, fearful, bold?
>
> **Interaction with Other Characters:** Is the character a leader or a follower? Friendly or unfriendly? Helpful or selfish?
>
> **Words and Actions:** How does the character respond to events and challenges?
>
> **Thoughts and Feelings:** What are the character's short- and long-term goals?
>
> **Conflict:** What threatens the character or stands in the way of his or her goals?

3. As a class, create a richly detailed physical description of a character. Ask students: *Is there something unusual about this character's appearance? What makes this character stand out?*

An eye patch? A limp? Beautiful hair? A great smile?

4. Next, build a personality for the character. Remind students that nobody's perfect, so give the character both positive *and* negative traits. Explain that someone who is very smart might have two "left feet," or the absent-minded teacher might be a great storyteller. Ask students to suggest a talent or talents that the character might have. Perhaps he can speak to horses, or she carves beautiful ice statues. Maybe he knows several languages, or she can read people's minds!

5. Invite the class to make suggestions about the character's goals. Ask: *What does this character want more than anything in the world? What must he or she do to achieve this goal? What is one thing the character has already accomplished? What is one thing he or she regrets?*

6. Complete the chart by having students decide on a name for the character. Mention that names can conjure an image. A surprising character name can add to the fun of a story! Ask students how they might picture a cowboy named Shakespeare or an alligator named Fluffy.

7. Finally, invite students to complete their own Character Chart about the main character of a story. Have them write a short story about this character.

8. When students are done, have them illustrate their stories and share them in small groups. Discuss how the Character Chart helped them create interesting characters.

Extended Learning

- Use the Character Chart to profile an antagonist. When the protagonist and antagonist are both profiled, ask students to write a dialogue between the two characters.

- Have students write a one-paragraph scene about their protagonist in a variety of circumstances, such as in a haunted house or at a surprise party.

- Ask students who like to read books in series to describe how the main character changed from the first book to the last. Some examples include: *A Series of Unfortunate Events, Harry Potter, Artemis Fowl, Chet Gecko,* and *The Sammy Keyes Mysteries.*

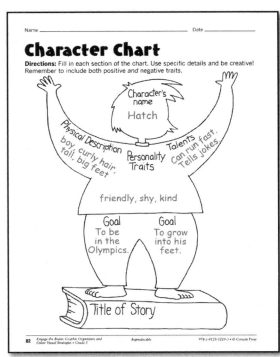

Name _____ Date _____

Character Chart

Directions: Fill in each section of the chart. Use specific details and be creative! Remember to include both positive *and* negative traits.

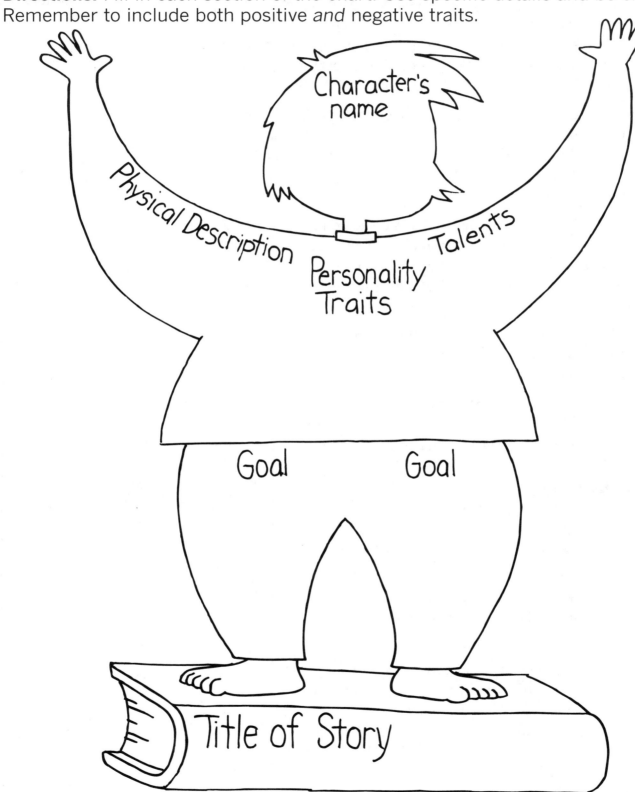

Building a Story: Story Analysis Map

Skills Objectives
Understand plot structure.
Identify the key characteristics of the mystery genre.

Materials
Lost Ticket Mystery reproducible

Building a Story reproducible

overhead projector and transparency

Mystery stories are very popular with young readers. A **Story Analysis Map** is a post-reading tool that can help students isolate the major elements of a story, such as a mystery. Completing a story analysis map increases overall comprehension and understanding of plot structure, and is ideal for small group discussions.

1. Have students raise their hands if they have ever read a mystery story. Encourage them to recommend their favorites, and write them on the board. Ask students to name some elements that make a story a mystery. For example: *something is missing; someone has a secret; something strange and unexplained is happening; there is some kind of puzzle to solve.*

2. Give students a copy of the **Lost Ticket Mystery** and **Building a Story reproducibles (pages 85–87)**. Have them take turns reading parts of the story until it is complete.

3. Place a transparency of the Building a Story reproducible on the overhead. Ask students: *Where did most of the story take place? When did the story take place?* Note anything unique about the setting. Write the answers on the map.

4. Then ask students to name the protagonist and antagonist in the story. Explain that the antagonist is anything or anyone in conflict with the protagonist. It may be another person or animal, nature, society, or fate. Point out that the conflict may also be internal. For "Lost Ticket Mystery," the protagonist is *Brooke* and the antagonist is *fate.*

5. Explain that conflict is the main problem the protagonist must face or solve. The complications that arise are the elements of rising action. Discuss how each element adds to the story. Write on the map: *Conflict/Problem: The winning lottery ticket is missing. Rising Action: The deadline for turning in the ticket is approaching. Brooke helps Mrs. Thomas search. Alex gives Brooke a clue.*

6. Point out that the climax of the story is not usually the end. It is the peak or turning point of the action. Encourage students to determine the turning point in the story. In this case, it is probably

when Brooke realizes where the ticket may be located. She runs to the library, gets the book, and opens it to find the ticket.

7. Help students understand falling action by asking: *Are there any explanations of the outcome after the climax? Does the author tie up any loose ends?* Record students' responses on the map. Finally, write the resolution or ending of the story. Ask students to read through their copy of the story and circle any clues that helped them find the answers.

8. Allow students to use their copy of the Building a Story reproducible to independently analyze another mystery story or a story from a different genre, such as fantasy or historical fiction.

Extended Learning

- Ask students to think about the kinds of words they might find in a mystery such as: *motive, evidence, red herring,* and *alibi.* Have students look up the words and make a Mystery Word Wall.

- Read aloud a mystery picture book from the *High-Rise Private Eyes* series by Cynthia Rylant. Invite students to point out the mystery elements throughout the book.

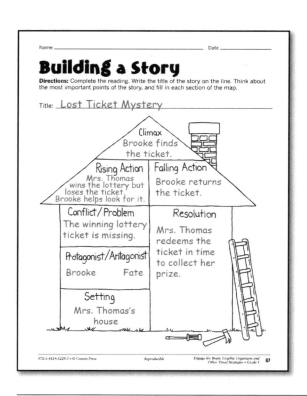

Lost Ticket Mystery

"Oh my gosh!" Brooke's mom sat up from her chair and held out the community section of the newspaper. "It says here that Mrs. Thomas is this week's big lottery winner!"

Brooke quickly scanned the article and grinned. "She won 20,000 dollars! I'm so happy for her!" During the summer Brooke often babysat for Mrs. Thomas when she went to work. Mrs. Thomas was a single mom with three children. Alex was Brooke's favorite. He was four and the opposite of his older brother and sister, Josh and Chandra. He was quiet and loved to sit inside with Brooke. He was just learning to read, so he spent a lot of time looking at his picture books and figuring out the text. Brooke enjoyed taking him to the library at his preschool, where he helped put books on the shelves.

On Monday morning, Brooke knocked at Mrs. Thomas's door. She was excited to hear the details of the big win.

"Hi Brooke," Chandra said gloomily when she answered. "My mom is in the kitchen."

"What's wrong?" Brooke asked as she walked inside. Mrs. Thomas looked up. It was easy to see she had been crying.

"It's terrible," she said. "I won the lottery. Now I can't find the ticket."

"Oh no. Don't you have the number?"

"Yes. I gave it to them over the phone to confirm that I had won," she replied. "But the rules say I have to turn in the ticket. I have to turn it in within three days or I forfeit the money. I have until three o'clock today. I've looked everywhere. Chandra and Josh helped me too. They are so disappointed. I'm glad I didn't say anything to Alex."

"Where do you think you put it?" Mrs. Thomas pointed to the basket by the phone. With her permission, Brooke sorted through the papers. There were business cards, postcards, and sale announcements. There were two letters in open envelopes. Brooke checked each to see if the ticket had slipped inside.

Alex ran into the kitchen. "Hi Brooke," he said giving her a hug. "I'm almost ready for school." He frowned. "What's the matter?"

"We lost something, honey," his mom said. "I'm sad that I can't find it."

The little boy agreed. "My teacher is sad when we can't find our library books. I never lose mine." He picked up a book from the counter. "This one is due today." The book fell to the floor. Brooke picked it up. Tucked inside the paper pocket on the inside cover there was an advertisement for a shoe sale.

"Alex, what do you do when you help your teacher in the library?" Brooke asked, her mind starting to whirl.

"I put reminder cards in the books."

"Like this?" Brooke slipped the ad from the paper pocket.

"Yes," Alex nodded.

Brooke was suddenly excited. "You brought a book back on Friday. Do you remember what it was called?"

"No. But it was about a pig. He was afraid to go to school."

"Mrs. Thomas, don't go anywhere. I have an idea. I'll be back as soon as I can." Her heart pounding, Brooke ran the two blocks to the preschool. Alex's teacher was already at her desk. "I'm sorry to bother you," Brooke gasped. "But I need to see a book in your library. I think it's called *Mommy Loves Owen.*"

The teacher found the book and Brooke held her breath. She opened the cover and slipped the lottery ticket from the paper pocket. She then thanked Alex's teacher and ran all the way back to Mrs. Thomas's house.

"I don't know how to thank you!" Mrs. Thomas exclaimed as Brooke handed her the ticket.

"I do," Alex smiled as he wrapped his arms around Brooke and gave her a big hug.

Name _____   Date _____

Building a Story

Directions: Complete the reading. Write the title of the story on the line. Think about the most important points of the story, and fill in each section of the map.

Title: _____

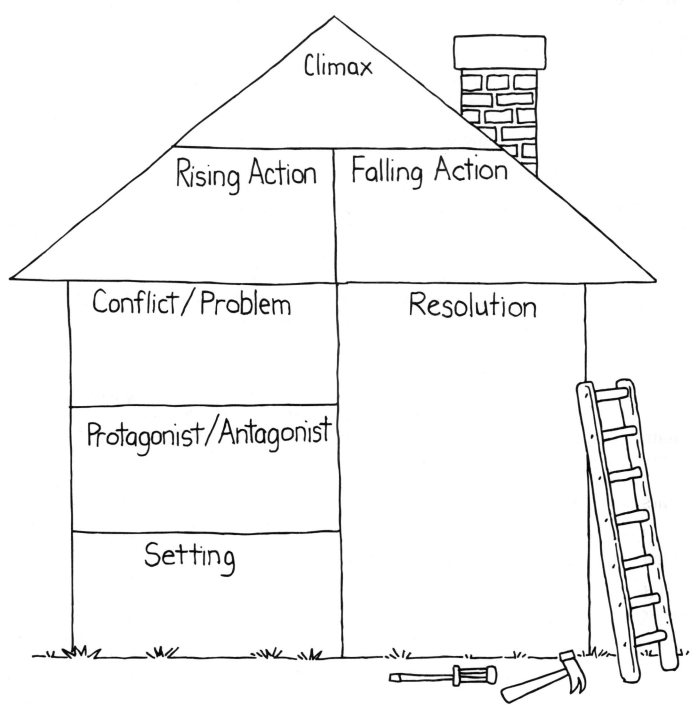

Climax

Rising Action   Falling Action

Conflict / Problem   Resolution

Protagonist / Antagonist

Setting

CHAPTER 5

Physical Education, Art, and Music

To Your Health: Bulletin Board

Skills Objectives
Read for a purpose.
Speak to an audience.
Communicate information visually.

Creating a display on the classroom **Bulletin Board** can provide reference support for students during reading and writing activities. It makes information accessible at all times, and acts as a simple "snapshot" to help students internalize the information shown.

1. Explain to students that we are each responsible for managing our own health. One way to do this is to stay informed. Ask: *What is a good way to find information about a health concern?* Answers might include: *Talk to a doctor or other health professional. Look up the information on the Internet.*

2. Tell students that they will make small posters to display on a bulletin board about staying healthy throughout the year. Separate the bulletin board into seasonal sections *winter, spring, summer,* and *fall.*

3. Invite students to brainstorm health issues or concerns that are specific to each season. For example, ask: *What are some dangers that are unique to the winter months?* Answers might include: *falling on ice, getting hurt while snowboarding, catching a cold or the flu, skating on unsafe ice and falling in, frostbite.*

4. Ask students: *What are some things you can do to prevent illness such as colds, or injury from falls or accidents?* Answers might include: *wash your hands often, get a flu shot, dress properly for the weather, wear safety equipment for sports, eat healthy meals, get enough sleep.*

5. Write students' answers on the board, and choose one to serve as an example. For example, ask what information would be useful for a poster on frostbite. Answers might include: *define frostbite, give tips on how to avoid it and treat it, give information such as hotlines.*

6. Have each student choose a health topic for an informational poster. Before students begin, ask them to take notes about what they already know and what they want to learn about the topic.

7. As they work, circulate around the room to make sure students are choosing appropriate examples. Encourage them to come up with interesting headings and include visual information such as charts, drawings, or photographs. Allow ample time for students to complete the assignment.

8. Display students' work on the bulletin board you have prepared. Allow time for each student to present his or her poster to the class. Invite the class to ask questions about the health topic. This will help you determine if the student understands the material.

Extended Learning

- Invite a health professional to come and speak to the class about health issues and ways to stay healthy.

- Ask students to look up the term *advocate*. Accept definitions such as: *spokesperson, supporter, promoter, crusader*. Have students research a well-known health advocate and present their findings to the class.

FROSTBITE

Wear a hat, hood, or scarf.

Wear layers of clothing.

Keep fingertips, earlobes, and nose covered when outside.

If a layer of clothing gets wet, remove it.

A Portable Gallery: Trading Cards

Materials

Trading Cards
reproducible

overhead projector
and transparency

Skills Objectives

Compare characteristics of artworks.
Understand that works of art have a history.
Research and summarize information.

Trading Cards are a part of popular culture, and so have a unique appeal to young learners. They help students to recall facts and details, and summarize data. Creating cards offers students a fun way to demonstrate their knowledge.

1. Ask students if they collect trading cards of any kind, such as baseball cards. Invite them to explain the elements that make up the cards, such as name, picture, biographical information, statistics, special skills or characteristics, and achievements.

2. Give students a copy of the **Trading Cards reproducible (page 92)**, and place a copy of the reproducible on the overhead. Tell them that they will make their own trading cards about famous works of art. On these cards, students will record similar information, detailing facts about the artwork and the artist.

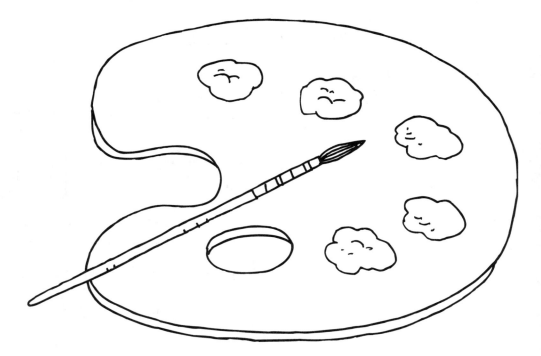

3. Discuss with students what they already know about art. Ask: *Does anyone have a favorite artist? Why do you like this artist's work? What are your favorite pieces of artwork?*

4. Choose a favorite piece of artwork to use for a sample trading card, such as the *Mona Lisa* by Leonardo da Vinci. Point out the information needed for the card. Tell students they will begin by tracing a copy of the artwork from a book, or cutting and pasting a photocopy. (Draw a simple replication on the transparency.) Note that some images may also be downloaded from the Internet.

5. Note that the information on the card includes the name of the painting, sculpture, or other artwork; the artist; style; date created; current location; and fun facts. Model how to fill in information on the trading card. Ask students what resources would be best for finding this information. *(books, videos, experts, the Internet)*

6. Give students time to research their chosen subjects. Point out that there are four cards on the page, so they need to choose four different subjects. Encourage students to choose different media, such as painting, sculpture, photography, jewelry, pottery, drawing, mosaic, and so on. Some of these media are more obscure, so it's okay if students only choose painting and sculpture, for example.

7. When the cards are completed, invite each student to present the facts about one of their artworks. Then ask students to circulate around the room and find students who made trading cards about the same artworks or artists. Encourage them to discuss why they chose these subjects and what they like about them.

Extended Learning

- Divide the class into student pairs. Have one student act as a famous artist (or subject in a painting), while his or her partner conducts an interview.

- If you have computer access, allow students to explore art history at the National Gallery of Art Web site: http://www.nga.gov/education/classroom/

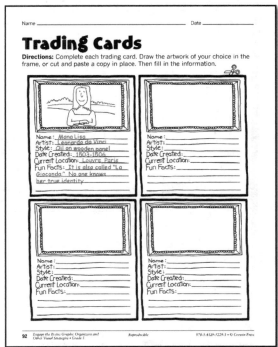

Trading Cards

Directions: Complete each trading card. Draw the artwork of your choice in the frame, or cut and paste a copy in place. Then fill in the information.

Name: _____
Artist: _____
Style: _____
Date Created: _____
Current Location: _____
Fun Facts: _____
_____
_____
_____

Name: _____
Artist: _____
Style: _____
Date Created: _____
Current Location: _____
Fun Facts: _____
_____
_____

Name: _____
Artist: _____
Style: _____
Date Created: _____
Current Location: _____
Fun Facts: _____
_____
_____

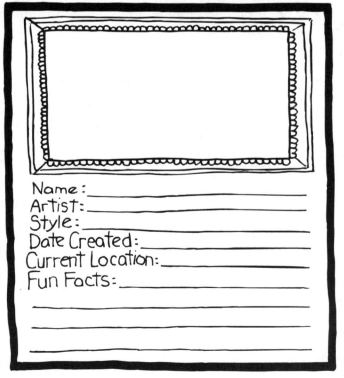

Name: _____
Artist: _____
Style: _____
Date Created: _____
Current Location: _____
Fun Facts: _____
_____
_____

Music to My Ears: Triple Venn Diagram

Skills Objectives
Use prior knowledge.
Compare and contrast data.
Discover relationships among topics.

Materials
Triple Venn Diagram reproducible

musical instruments or pictures of instruments

CDs or audiotapes of zydeco, bluegrass, and ragtime music (optional)

CD or cassette player (optional)

A **Triple Venn Diagram** is a graphic organizer that helps students compare and contrast information about three different subjects. In the course of a music unit, this organizer is an excellent tool for comparing different music genres. Insights learned can lead to a deeper understanding of music in relation to history and culture.

1. Introduce the concept of "compare and contrast" by holding up two musical instruments (or pictures) such as a clarinet and a violin. Ask students: *How are these instruments alike? How are they different?* For example: *Both are musical instruments. Both are in the orchestra. One is a woodwind; one is a strings instrument. One is played by blowing through it; one is played with a bow.*

2. Remind students that a typical Venn diagram has two circles and is used to compare two different things. Draw two intersecting circles on the board. Tell students that they are going to use a *triple* Venn diagram to compare and contrast *three* different things. Draw a third intersecting circle on the board.

3. Work together as a class to compare three different forms of American music. Ask students to share what they know about different music genres, such as classical, rock and roll, rhythm and blues, rap, jazz, reggae, and so on.

4. Share with students the following facts about three different forms of American music—zydeco, bluegrass, and ragtime. If you wish, play recordings of zydeco, bluegrass, and ragtime, so students can compare what they hear as well.

Zydeco
Originated: Early 20th century among Creole people of Louisiana
Signature: Heavily syncopated, fast tempo
Instruments: Accordian, rub-board, fiddle, guitar, bass guitar, drums
Performer: Boozoo Chavis recorded "Paper in My Shoe"

Bluegrass

Originated: 1940s Kentucky, roots in English, Irish, and Scottish traditional music

Signature: Melody instruments take turns playing improvised solos while the others play backup

Instruments: Fiddle, banjo, acoustic guitar, mandolin, upright bass, resonator guitar

Performer: Bill Monroe's band The Blue Grass Boys

Ragtime

Originated: First published in Kansas City in 1897, peak popularity between 1899 and 1918

Signature: Usually written in 2/4 or 4/4 time

Instruments: Piano

Performer: Scott Joplin, composer/pianist known as the "King of Ragtime"

5. Model how to use the triple Venn diagram to compare these three genres. In the center, where the circles overlap, write how the genres are alike: *American styles of music.* Have students suggest contrasting facts for the outer circles. For example, there is a different performer noted for each type of music.

6. The most complex areas of the diagram are where the circles overlap each other. Point out that these sections create a space to compare the subjects in pairs. For example: Zydeco/Bluegrass: *fiddle, guitar, fast tempos*; Zydeco/Ragtime: *syncopated*; Bluegrass/Ragtime: *roots in traditional folk music.*

7. Give students a copy of the **Triple Venn Diagram reproducible (page 95)**. Make sure they understand how to record similar and contrasting information. Have students complete their diagrams, comparing three different music genres of their choice. If you have computer access, invite students to conduct research at the Open Directory Project: *http://dmoz.org/Arts/Music/Styles*.

8. Display the finished diagrams on a bulletin board featuring information and pictures about American music.

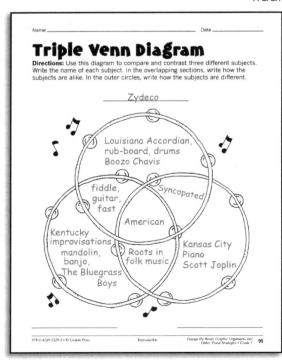

Triple Venn Diagram

Directions: Use this diagram to compare and contrast three different subjects. Write the name of each subject. In the overlapping sections, write how the subjects are alike. In the outer circles, write how the subjects are different.

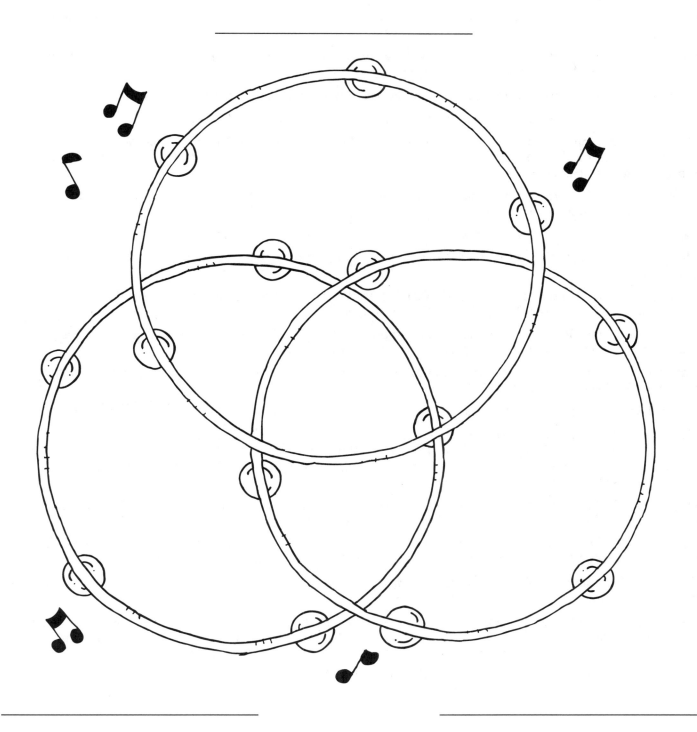

References

Akers, S. (2003). *Understanding equivalent fractions*. Retrieved December 6, 2006, from Help with Fractions Web site: http://www.helpwithfractions.com/equivalent-fractions.html.

Barton, B. *Graphic organizers*. (n.d.). Retrieved August 10, 2006, from The Science Classroom at Mohave High School Web site: http://gotoscience.com/Graphic_Organizers.html#Toppage.

Bromley, K., Irwin-De Vitis, L., & Modlo, M. (1995). *Graphic organizers: Visual strategies for active learning*. New York, NY: Scholastic Professional Books.

Byers, J. (n.d.). *Instructional methods: Graphic organizers*. Retrieved August 15, 2006, from the Instructional Strategies Online, Saskatoon Public Schools, Inc. Web site: http://olc.spsd.sk.ca/DE/PD/instr/strats/graphicorganizers.

Education World. (n.d.). *National standards*. Retrieved November 30, 2006, from http://www.education-world.com/standards/national.

Forte, I., & Schurr, S. (2001). *Standards-based language arts graphic organizers, rubrics, and writing prompts for middle grade students*. Nashville, TN: Incentive Publications, Inc.

Gardner, H. (1983). *Frames of mind: The theory of multiple intelligences*. New York, NY: Basic Books.

Graphic.org. (n.d.). *Graphic organizers*. Retrieved August 10, 2006, from http://www.graphic.org.

Hall, T., & Strangman, N. (2002). *Graphic organizers*. Wakefield, MA: National Center on Accessing the General Curriculum. Retrieved August 15, 2006, from the CAST: Universal Design for Learning Web site: http://www.cast.org/publications/ncac/ncac_go.html.

Hopkins, G. (2003). *Debates in the classroom*. Retrieved September 20, 2006, from the Education World Web site: http://www.education-world.com/a_curr/strategy/strategy012.shtml.

Jensen, E., & Johnson, G. (1994). *The learning brain*. San Diego, CA: Turning Point for Teachers.

McCarthy, Bernice. (1990). Using the 4MAT system to bring learning styles to schools. *Educational Leadership, 48* (2), 31–37.

National Council for the Social Studies. (2002). *Expectations of excellence: Curriculum standards for social studies*. Silver Spring, MD: National Council for the Social Studies (NCSS).

National Council of Teachers of English and International Reading Association. (1996). *Standards for the English language arts*. Urbana, IL: National Council of Teachers of English (NCTE).

National Council of Teachers of Mathematics. (2005). *Principles and standards for school mathematics*. Reston, VA: National Council of Teachers of Mathematics (NCTM).

National Research Council. (2005). *National science education standards*. Washington, DC: National Academy Press.

Novak, J. D., & Cañas, A. J. (2006, December 12). *The theory underlying concept maps and how to construct them*. Technical Report IHMC CmapTools 2006-01, Florida Institute for Human and Machine Cognition. Retrieved August 15, 2006, from the IHMC CmapTools Web site: http://cmap.ihmc.us/Publications/ResearchPapers/TheoryCmaps/TheoryUnderlyingConceptMaps.htm.

Ogle, D. M. (2000). Make it visual: A picture is worth a thousand words. In M. McLaughlin & M. Vogt (Eds.), *Creativity and innovation in content area teaching*. Norwood, MA: Christopher-Gordon.

Perlman, H. (2006, August 28). *Earth's water distribution*. Retrieved November 3, 2006, from the United States Geological Survey Web site: http://ga.water.usgs.gov/edu/waterdistribution.

Scavo, T. (1997, August 3). *Geoboards in the classroom*. Retrieved December 7, 2006, from the Math Forum Web site: http://mathforum.org/trscavo/geoboards/.

Seevers, J. (n.d.). *Strategies for accessing the social studies curriculum: Graphic organizers*. Retrieved August 15, 2006, from the Special Connections, University of Kansas Web site: http://www.specialconnections.ku.edu/cgi-bin/cgiwrap/specconn/main.php?cat=instruction&section=main&subsection=ss/graphic.

Tate, M. L. (2003). *Worksheets don't grow dendrites: 20 Instructional strategies that engage the brain*. Thousand Oaks, CA: Corwin Press.